A LONG SLOW WALK FROM THE STATION

The Story of
Brocton Prisoner of War Camp
1917 - 1919

ISBN 978-0-9527247-9-7

Printed by Russell Press, Nottingham

Contents

Introduction

2014 saw the centenary of the start of the Great War, and the anniversary was commemorated in many ways by local communities all over Britain. Berkswich History Society published a book "Memories – Berkswich in the Great War" and in the course of researching that book it was discovered that the Commandant of the Prisoner of War Camp at Brocton, Sir Arthur Grant, had brought his family to live in the Parish. I wanted to find out more, but very little appears to have been published about any German Prisoner of War Camps in the UK. I set out to discover what I could with help from several more scholarly people than myself. Special thanks must go to Sir Archibald Grant, grandson of the Camp Commandant, who kindly allowed me access to his grandfather's diaries.

Brocton Prisoner of War Camp is just as much part of our local history as are the stories of the soldiers who trained on Cannock Chase prior to fighting in France. What sort of lives did the Prisoners lead, and how did they fill their time as they waited, hopefully, to return home?

Over 200 Germans, mainly young men between the ages of 18 and 30, died in the Camp, either from their wounds or victims of the influenza epidemic which swept through the country in 1918. They are buried in our Parish in Cannock Chase War Cemetery.

This book is the result of my research into the Camp at Brocton from 1917 – 1919. It is not an academic thesis but an account of life in Camp and how it touched the lives of local people.

Many families have stories about relatives who trained on the Chase during World War I, but few know about the Prisoner of War Camp. I hope this book will help keep alive the memory of all the men who lived for a short time in the Parish of Berkswich, whatever their nationality.

Beryl Holt

Chairman, Berkswich History Society.
2015

POW

From a collection of poems entitled "14" by
Staffordshire Poet Laureate 2013 -14 Tom Wyre.
The poems were specially commissioned to commemorate
the centenary of WW1

Conscripted by circumstances,
Funnelled into a war spun web,
I had no choice.
I trained to be a teacher,
A true calling,
Nein, Nein, No.
In fact I know I am a teacher,
Chalks and blackboards borrowed for other lessons.
I teach history, now assured that we never learn.
Handed a rifle, ordered into uniform,
Now swapped for another.
From Dusseldorf, my name is Franz.
Not Fritz, Kraut or Hun,
Not someone choosing to shoot or bomb you into a box.
How the hell did the sky turn upside down?
Rattle me and spit me out to sit here as a prisoner,
In Brocton's tree lined bars and cross wires,
Under a tower's beady eye.
I've given up one set of chains for another yoke;
On a farm, replacing horses, I plough this field,
Digging other trenches, but at least the air is clean here,
Free from mustard and here the birds sing.
The unnatural quiet of the Western Front,
Yells loudly in between pounding shells,
More so since the birds have flown.

I am a man of words,
Now my tongue sleeps,
Lost for them.
A man and not a number,
A prisoner of conscience,
Haunted by men marching towards me in rows,
Laughing and singing those first days,
Buttons polished like suns.
For all of the world,
Their dreams in their kitbags left behind,
They just walked towards me and stared,
Pipes playing in the air.
I might as well have shot at mirrors,
Taunted always by the pull of triggers.

My innocence cracked as I also died that day,
Inside I knew wrong, but instincts are strong,
For preservation, my soul sold out,
Clambering from an open box.

I have three loves back home,
My wife, my mother and my fatherland.
My biggest love here is my love of life.

I'm now here until the end,
At least until the bug strikes,
As I say to you,
I just wanted to be a teacher.

Chapter 1

Cannock Chase, Staffordshire

In the centre of England, sandwiched between the industrial areas of the Potteries and the Black Country, is a beautiful area of open heathland known as Cannock Chase. In 1873 the Chase had been used for large-scale exercises involving cavalry, artillery and infantry units of the Regular Army. Again in 1897 volunteer units used the area for military manoeuvres but, in the spring of 1914, all was quiet and the Chase was an area of recreation for the people of Stafford and the surrounding area.

Donkeys on Milford Common ready for the Fair

Trains crowded with people arrived at Milford and Brocton Station throughout the summer with everyone hoping to enjoy the fresh air and sunshine. A fair appeared on Milford Common each Easter, Whitsun and August Bank Holidays bringing swing boats, hobby-horses, coconut shies and other attractions. After a picnic, families would gather blackberries and bilberries, as cows and sheep wandered through the bracken-covered hills. Early morning visitors, or those walking at dusk, might just catch a glimpse of a group of fallow deer - if they proceeded quietly!

Workmen who built the Military Camps

Each winter children would delight in sledging down Spring Hill or the surrounding gentler slopes on to Milford Common while perhaps their parents enjoyed a drink in the warmth of the Barley Mow.

A golf club had opened at Milford in 1894 after Dr Reid, the local GP, had negotiated with Thomas Anson, the Earl of Lichfield from nearby Shugborough Hall, to rent part of the Chase at Milford for one shilling a year. A lunch was held at the Barley Mow, to inaugurate the new nine hole course, before members took part in their very first competition.[1]

---

[1] 100 Years of Golf

Over the years the membership had continued to grow and it had become a thriving club. But things were to change dramatically with the outbreak of war in August 1914.

In December, 1914, agreement was finally reached between the Earl of Lichfield and the War Office to construct a camp on the Earl's land on Cannock Chase.[2] Designated as a training camp for recruits to the British Army, the Camp was begun early in 1915 and before long the first soldiers began to arrive.

Brocton Camp

As the war progressed things changed, there was a need for more accommodation for captured soldiers and by August 1916, the War Office had decided to establish a Detention Camp for German Prisoners of War on the Chase. They wrote to inform the Earl of Lichfield of their intentions. His agent replied by saying "His offer of the free use of the land in question was made for the sole purpose of training the troops for the war and no other purpose whatsoever.

[2] Ref D615/ES/6/10 Staffordshire Record Office

Lord Lichfield wishes to protest most strongly against the ground being made use of for any other object. He begs that this protest may be at once laid before the Army Council".[3] After being informed that the Prisoners of War would be housed in existing huts and that the decision of the War Office did not entail any additional huts being built or any more ground taken, the Earl eventually agreed to the arrival of the Germans. It was also pointed out to the Earl that, in time of war, the powers that be could do almost anything they thought appropriate!

Early in 1917, it was decided that lines "A", "B", "C", "E" and "F" - originally built to house the 1st and 2nd Infantry Brigades - should be turned into the Prisoner of War Camp for up to a maximum of 6,000 prisoners. Lines "A", "B" and "C" were a quarter of a mile to the east of Lines "E" and "F" and separated by the Military Railway, which had recently been constructed from the main line station at Milford, across Milford Common, over land belonging to the Sister Dora Convalescent Home and then up on to the top of the Chase. This railway was not used to carry passengers, but to transport supplies and equipment for the thousands of men who would be living and training in the Camps.

The first prisoners would reach Milford in April 1917, but before their arrival it was necessary to appoint a Commandant to take control of the Camp.

[3] Ref D615/EA/36 Staffordshire Record Office.

Chapter 2

The Commandant

Lieutenant Colonel Arthur Grant was the elder son of Sir Arthur Henry Grant, 9th Baronet of Monymusk in Aberdeenshire. He was born on 14th September, 1879, and educated at Eton before embarking on a career in the Army in 1899, serving with the 12th (Prince of Wales's Royal) Lancers. In August 1902, the 23 year old returned to his ancestral home after spending over four eventful years fighting in South Africa.

Monymusk House, Ancestral Home of the Grant Family since 1713.

The tenants on the estate had celebrated his coming of age very quietly in September 1900, while he was still fighting the Boers. They had considered it unseemly to make merry whilst the heir to the estate was in such danger but, on his return, there was much rejoicing at his homecoming.

While in South Africa, Arthur had been in hospital three times; once with jaundice and twice he was found to be suffering from typhoid fever. On another occasion he was ambushed by Boers. After shooting two of them dead, he was captured and held in a nearby house. When he awoke next morning he discovered that his captors had fled during the night, leaving him alone with the bodies of the two men he had killed. After burying the dead, he returned to his company, none the worse for his adventure.[4] He was created a Companion of the Distinguished Service Order "In recognition of services during the operations in South Africa".[5]

After a spell at home he travelled to India and by May 1904, he had been promoted to Captain. Five years later, on 25th September, 1909, he retired owing to ill health - a legacy from his time in South Africa, followed by a slight stroke, which he suffered whilst in India. It was agreed that he would take over the running of the Monymusk estate and his parents would retire to England. On 12th October, less than three weeks after his retirement from the Army, Arthur married Evelyn (Evie) Alice Lindsay Wood.

The story is told of how the couple met. Arthur was on leave from his army duty in India and was on his way home to Monymusk. His train became snow-bound at Bridge of Allan, a town near Freeland, just south of Perth. A friend who arrived by a later train found Arthur in the station's

[4] Aberdeen Journal 18th August 1902

[5] London Gazette 26th June, 1902

waiting room, wondering what to do next. The friend told Arthur that he had been invited to a ball at Freeland and he was sure that an extra guest would not be unwelcome. After all, anything was better than sitting on his suitcase in the station waiting room! So in borrowed finery, he set off for the ball. At dinner, he sat next to one of the daughters of the House. After the usual Victorian courtship during which Evie was chaperoned every time she met Arthur, they eventually married and were blissfully happy

Freedland House, home of Evelyn Grant nee Wood

In April 1912 Captain Arthur Grant became a Lieutenant Colonel of the 5th Battalion (Buchan and Formartin) Gordon Highlanders and in May 1915, he accompanied the Battalion to France leaving his wife behind with four young children.

Arthur Grant was wounded by a shell whilst returning from the support trenches to Battalion Headquarters on the morning of 18th June 1915. The wounds to his arm and back were severe enough to result in his being invalided home. After a spell in the Duchess of Westminster Hospital at Le Tourquet, he returned to Britain to recuperate but he was never again considered fit enough to return to the Front. He would suffer considerable pain as a result of his injuries for the rest of his life. He would tell a young cousin that it felt as though his finger nails were constantly being pulled out.

Sir Arthur, Lady Evelyn & Dyonése Levett
Pictured sometime around 1925

On 1st March 1917 he succeeded to the title of 10th Baronet Grant of Monymusk and Cullen, on the death of his father. Then on 28th March 1917, following a spell at the camp for German Prisoners of War and civilian internees in Handforth, Cheshire, he was appointed Commandant of the Prisoner of War Camp which was due to open in April 1917 at Brocton on Cannock Chase, in the heart of rural Staffordshire.

Chapter 3

Arrivals

Sir Arthur was instructed to report to Brocton on Wednesday 10th April, 1917 along with one interpreter, 2nd Lieutenant Harold George Theodosius, son of the former vicar of Ranton, a small village three and a half miles west of Stafford. Before joining the army Harold had been employed as Bursar at King Edward VII School in Lytham St Annes.

Sir Arthur sent his trusted Adjutant[6], Alfred Birley, ahead of him. Birley knew just how a prisoner of war camp should be run as he had spent time as a prisoner of the Germans, and he was certain that things should be done differently in England!

Birley told the story of his imprisonment and escape to Sir Arthur when he was appointed his Adjutant. He had been captured on 29th October 1914 near Ypres and on the way to the prison camp in Westphalia they were pretty roughly treated. "One night 53 of us were locked in a church, and had nothing to eat for over 24 hours. At last they emptied a basket of mouldy bread on the floor, and left us a bucket of water. We were then crammed into a closed railway van for 56 hours. Only once were we allowed to get out and that for just a few minutes. For food we had some scraps of bread.

[6] A military officer who acts as an administrative assistant to a senior officer.

I made several plans for escaping but never found the right opportunity, and then I was transferred to another camp. Escape was not an easy matter as we were surrounded by high barbed wire fencing. On each of its four sides a sentry was posted, and at night four acetylene lamps lit the whole of the camp. The great night came, I waited till one of the sentries had his back turned, and then wriggled on my stomach to the fencing. I managed to sever one strand of the fence, the twang of it made the greatest noise I've ever heard! But the sentry walked on. I snapped the second strand, which made an awful noise. Still the sentry walked on. I crawled under the wire and on for 100 yards before there was any shelter. Then I moved away as quickly as I could without making a sound.

The only food I had was a few biscuits and a little chocolate. Whenever I approached a farm the dogs always smelt or heard me. For three days my only food was apples stolen from the farm orchards.

It wasn't safe to travel by day and although I had plenty of tobacco, it was not even safe to enjoy a smoke as the smell of tobacco might easily put an inquisitive German on my track. One day my hiding place was the side of a cliff, crouched underneath a thin bush. Two elderly Germans came to the top of the cliff to admire the view. If they had looked down I would have been spotted. On another occasion I hid in the rushes of a river and, coming out too soon, had to pass the time of day with some workmen.

When I actually crossed the frontier into Holland I was in a pretty bad condition: cramped with sleeping out in the wet, my feet swollen and bleeding, I could hardly stand. That first Dutch farmhouse was a godsend."[7]

Sir Arthur knew that he would be able rely on such a man, and his experience would be invaluable in the coming months. They would treat their German prisoners with more respect than Birley had received in enemy hands.

Arriving at Brocton Sir Arthur discovered he had just 35 sentries available to keep control of the Camp - not a lot for 24 hour surveillance. He must instigate some rules. Although it would seem obvious that the aim was to keep the Prisoners in the Camp, Sir Arthur set to and wrote his "Orders for Sentries".

Sir Arthur Grant

1. The main object to be studied is not to allow a prisoner to escape.

2. To be smart and alert whilst on sentry duty and not to lounge about

3. Not on any account to converse with the prisoners, or any individuals, civilians, or persons in uniform.

4. To keep secret the countersign (password) if in operation, and if not given correctly the person

[7] Bases on a report in the Dorking Advertiser 2nd October, 1915

to be detained and the Guard Commander informed.

5. Not to give any information to anyone except your own officers.

6. Sentries will carry 10 rounds of ammunition loose. One round will be carried in the belt or end of pouch and it must be easily accessible.

7. Sentries will not load until after challenging and not receiving a satisfactory answer.

8. Sentries may fire on any Prisoner of War they believe to be escaping, but on no other occasion except by order of an officer.

9. They must pay proper compliments to all officers according to rank. Sentries in lookout boxes will salute the Commandant by coming smartly to attention. They will not present arms.

10. Sentries will challenge all persons approaching their post between dusk and reveille.

11. It is distinctly understood that any prisoner attempting to pass the boundary fence (white posts with wire) or to go out through any gate without a permit signed by the Commandant will be fired on after being once warned and disregarding that warning.[8]

Sir Arthur discovered that he had a very nice bungalow situated just outside the wire and, he said, "With the most glorious view in England spread out before me." Although the view was delightful, the local wild life, from time to time,

---

[8] Ref 345/1418 National Records of Scotland

annoyed him. The cuckoos sang incessantly in the spring, and in November a fallow deer buck would regularly come and roar outside his window all night!

Like the prisoners, he was to feel the cold and he sent an urgent request to his wife for a hot water bottle! Still he did not sleep easily; his nights were often disturbed by the sound of gun fire and bombs exploding as the training of British soldiers, sometimes with live ammunition, continued on the Chase. Just for a moment or two he would be back in the trenches.

The hot water bottle took the chill off the cool April nights but by December things were rather different. Lying in bed under 4 blankets covered by an Army Great Coat together with his plaid and wearing his hat Sir Arthur was still freezing. As the snow lay on the ground the Commandant sent a message home to Monymusk asking for his old African Kaross,[9] and only when that had arrived did he feel warm enough to sleep soundly. By February he was feeling the cold again. He wrote in his pocket diary "Last April I ordered some coal to come in for the winter. But there isn't an ounce of it left not a splinter. I have such a big office it takes all the coal."

As he was not fully fit, he was required to attend regular Medical Boards and they said he was only to undertake light duties. Somehow this did not seem to fit with the ten hour day, six and a half day week, he was working. Many of his staff had been injured in some way or other and were not able to work to their full potential.

---

[9] A **kaross** is a cloak made of animal hide, with the hair left on, worn by the Khoikhoi peoples of S. Africa.

Captain Egerton reported for duty just days after the camp opened, but he has been shot in the head and partially paralysed and so could not do very much.

Although Sir Arthur had drawn up regulations for his sentries, he was also subject to a long list of Do's and Don'ts. The list seemed to be unending, but every aspect of his command was covered and he felt it was important that discipline was upheld at all times.

Prisoner inspects the list of rules!

Reproduced courtesy of R. Pursehouse

1. The Commandant should avoid familiarity with PoWs but should see that they are properly fed, housed, clothed, doctored and paid when entitled to pay.

2. PoWs should be punished severely for faults, after due investigation. It has been found a good plan to remit a day's punishment for good behaviour in prison or on fatigues.

3. The Commandant should always be cleanly and smartly dressed in the Lines.

4. The Commandant should frequently inspect all parts of the camp, and also the work of any working parties that may be out in the neighbourhood. He should occasionally go round camp at odd times of the night or early morning.

5. PoWs should be encouraged to occupy themselves in pursuits which do nobody any harm such as Band, Theatricals, Woodworking, Gardening, Lectures and Classes, Massage, Football, Reading. PoWs may be allowed to go for walks in the country when well behaved, and under proper guard.

6. PoWs should pay proper compliments to all officers and should be properly dressed on formed up and on marched off the various parades. PoWs must not smoke in the Pay or other offices.

7. No unauthorised person should talk to, or have any communication with, PoWs. A Commandant should be careful that the guards do not become too familiar with PoWs, or be bribed to pass in clothes, drink etc. or to make communication with other people. Women must not be allowed in or near the Camp.

8. Visitors who come merely out of curiosity should be kept at a distance.

9. Civilians who work in the Camp should be of known antecedents, and a system of "passes" registered by or applied for through the Commandant should be instigated.

10. A Commandant should endeavour to maintain friendly relations both with those officers who have to work with him and with the officers of the many departments with whom he will have correspondence.

11. PoWs may have 10/- per week or, if N.C.O's, £1 per week from their private monies.

12. PoWs should always be carefully searched on arriving at a camp and any articles such as Big Knives (small ones may be allowed), Cameras, Field Glasses, Maps, Compasses, Arms, Wire Cutters, Electric Torches, should be confiscated, together with any other articles at the discretion of the Commandant. Larger sums of money should also be withheld and a receipt given.

13. Telegrams ready to be filled in should be kept addressed to those concerned in case of the escape of a PoW. The same on recapture, as much trouble is thus avoided for those who are searching for escapees.

14. The Camp Police should inspect the perimeter of the Camp daily.

15. The guard should occasionally be tested by means of a false alarm.

16 The Commandant should draw up redress for guards and sentries in conjunction with the Operations General.

17. The Commandant is responsible for PoWs and must see that the Guard Officers act under his orders.

18. At the same time the Guard Officers are responsible that PoWs do not escape.

19. It is distinctly understood that the Commandant is the real head of the Camp and not the Guard Officers.

20. For Room and Hut inspections a definite plan should be laid down, shown to all comers, and insisted on. Worn out material should be shown to the 2nd Lieutenant and exchanged on 1 day weekly. The same to apply to clothing and the officer concerned should see the PoW does not obtain more than he ought, nor sell or otherwise dispose of articles at every opportunity. They are not very particular as to telling the truth.

21. Great care should be taken that there is no swindling or trading done by the cooks, as this sometimes occurs and naturally may be the cause of great dissatisfaction. The NCO's are also inclined to keep the best portions for themselves. This should be strenuously prevented and a fair and proper distribution made. This is particularly the case with Germans, though not unknown amongst others.

22. All drains and sluices to be kept scrupulously clean. Sand and waste must be removed as often as necessary and buried. All manhole covers should be removed at least once a week to allow bad gas to escape to ensure that the drains are in working order. A party of PoWs should be held-off for this, under supervision of an English pioneer. The PoW pioneers should also be the Fire Post and should be drilled and tested in this work. The Camp police should all know

the positions of fire buckets, hydraulic hoses, and ample Fire Orders should be drawn up and tested. A few PoWs should be held-off for light gardening work in the lines. This is found to greatly improve the appearance of the camp and also is very good exercise for convalescent men.

23. A general supervision of all funds should be exercised by the Commandant. But the actual charge of them should be undertaken by the 2nd in Command when there is one at a Camp. All monies should go through the various banking accounts and all books should be carefully checked from time to time. Boards of Audit should be held at the proper time.[10]

As well as setting out rules, there were several basic routine housekeeping matters to attend to such as ordering wooden drinking beakers and bowls. Sir Arthur also wrote and asked his wife, Evie, who was in London, to get him a cornet, with which they could signal lights out and reveille each day. Evie reported that she had managed to locate a new cornet for the princely sum of £4.4.0d. It would be engraved once she had the go ahead from her husband to purchase it.

While she was in London she also called on Dr Karl Markel. Dr Markel had been born in Germany in 1860 and, after completing his academic studies; he came to

[10] Doc, 6821 Imperial War Museum

Warrington to work for Joseph Crosfield & Sons Ltd., a company manufacturing soaps, glycerine and caustic soda.

After a short time he was promoted to a director of the company and in 1887 became a British citizen. In January the following year he married Ada Taylor at St Clement Danes, London.

Dr Markel

Well before the start of war, Karl worked to promote Anglo-German friendship but, at the outbreak of war, by which time the Markel family were living in London, he found his loyalty split between the country of his birth and his adopted home. Throughout the war, working from his house at 20 Queen's Gate Terrace, he funded comforts such as musical instruments, books, games, and medical equipment for German Prisoners of War and Internees in Great Britain. In 1917 his organisation was spending an average of £3,000 a month, this amount soon reached £4,500 a month. He was the official representative of the German Red Cross in England.

Evie wrote to her husband on 26th April, to say that she had visited Dr Markel[11] earlier in the day and he reported that he had heard from Arthur. She went on to say "Apparently you must make definite demands for things

[11] After the War Dr Markel set up a foundation to aid needy & worthy children in Germany who had suffered as a result of the war.

and fill in one of his forms for each request you make. A chest of games has already been sent off to you. He rambled on about what a lot of good work he is doing and how very delicate his position is and how he gets abused and yet how much the Foreign Office appreciate him. He was so German!" Although he was a British citizen, Dr Markel's permit which allowed him to visit camps had been withdrawn in 1916 and there were insinuations made in the House of Commons in November 1917 suggesting that he may be a spy!

Sir Arthur's first few days were spent in inspecting the various lines which, in his opinion, had not been left in a very desirable state when vacated by the previous tenants. He also toured the area getting his bearings, looking at the Power Station, the pumps and the wells, which, although they were 250 feet deep, did not produce enough water for all the camps.

The arrival of the first prisoners at Brocton was recorded in the local paper, although it was very careful not to mention the name of the camp or the railway station. The locals were not keen to have Germans on their doorstep!

"The weather was bitterly cold and occasional snow showers rendered waiting for the train a non-too attractive pastime. Many of the prisoners – there were several hundred in all – were wounded and arrangements had to be made for the transport of such men who could not walk. There were many pairs of crutches to be seen but, by means of private motor cars, a motor bus and army transport waggons, the journey to the camp was completed with ease. There were many lads among the prisoners and also some whom I should have classed as over military age. Most of the men appeared serious, some looked too ill to care, while some – evidently bent on making the best of life as it happened to be – were laughing and joking. One wounded officer in a car smiled cheerily and waved his hand to a batch of men in a transport waggon as he raced quickly by. But the laughers and jokers were in the minority – war had been no laughing matter to most of them. When the wounded had been sent on, the march of the main body began. Carrying their meagre belongings, it seemed *a long, slow walk from the station.* Well-guarded by soldiers with fixed bayonets, the procession ambled on, no soldierly dignity being shown by the prisoners, who marched awkwardly, without discipline, as though they were unwilling warriors. Perhaps they were."[12]

Milford & Brocton station

[12] Staffordshire Advertiser 14th April 1917.

William Mynors, land agent at Ingestre, also recorded in his diary the arrival of the prisoners. He estimated that about 300 arrived on 10th April, with another 500 arriving a week later. From the start of the year the Mynors family, living close to the Chase in Holdiford Road, had watched with interest, the erection of the fence and barbed wire around the huts that were to become the PoW Camp. William commented that escape would not be easy.[13]

Another prisoner wrote about his arrival at Camp. "We arrived in Brocton at 1 o'clock. Naturally, our life began with fun and games as our rations, which had been sent from Handforth, went astray and we never saw them again! Brocton is a very large camp consisting of compounds which are divided from one another. We were lucky in getting new blankets, but only received old washed straw-sacks.

Otherwise, the camp was well arranged. Regarding food, everything was thrown into one pot, but the bread and cakes were better even than in Handforth. We received cigarettes every ten days, only 10 oz. Drinks were not to be had for love or money."

The Prisoners were treated well - in stark contrast to the way our boys were treated by the Germans. Staffordshire lad, William Unett, wrote to his family once he was out of Germany and interred in Holland, telling of his experiences. "At Cambrai we were halted in the street outside the station by a drunken Bavarian who used the butt end of his rifle on some of us. We then started our journey into Germany and for three days all we were given was one meal on the

[13] Diary of William Mynors.

evening of our second day. Thanks to forethought in buying biscuits at Le Cateau before starting and the kindness of our guard, our compartment got sufficient food. I fear the wounded suffered greatly during the journey. We reached Torgau in the evening. Tired and stiff we emerged from the train. There was a feeble laugh from someone and one of the crowd of Germans in the station said "You will not laugh when you are outside". Have you ever heard a football crowd shout from a short distance off? Well, that was what we heard, and then we marched through a gap in the crowd, who cursed us, struck us, kicked us and spat with great accuracy and judgement. Our guards marched alongside, not dreaming of interfering. The colonels and senior officers being at the head of the column got most of the kicks. Those at the rear being more fortunate."[14]

The Bakery at Brocton Camp

It was clear to Sir Arthur that, with so many men in such a confined space, it was important that discipline was maintained. In January 1918 he was joined by Major George

[14] D3610/19/7/1 Staffordshire Record Office

C.B Musgrave, who had been wounded at Suola Bay, Gallipoli in 1917, whilst serving with the 6th Royal Inneskilling Fusiliers, but who was now capable of taking on the duties of the Assistant Commandant. During the next two years they would find their command and regulations would be tested to the limit.

Dyonése Levett recalls the day Sir Arthur visited Milford Hall for the very first time. "It was shortly after my brother had been killed and mother was lying in the Orangery resting. Suddenly there was a complete stranger at the door; a Scotchman obviously, kilted up, glengarry[15] askew. He said he had been appointed Commandant of the German Prisoner of War Camp and he wished to call upon and get to know all his neighbours. From that moment he became our dearest friend and was a regular visitor to Milford Hall." He often joined a shoot with Captain Levett or called on Mrs Levett for afternoon tea.

Cynthia Allsopp

When in London he would take Dyonése Levett, who was at school in

[15] The glengarry is a traditional Scots cap made of thick-milled woollen material with ribbons hanging down behind. It is normally worn as part of Scottish military or civilian Highland dress,

Brondesbury, out to a lovely restaurant, shouting out "Off the chain" to his wife as they left the house. He also visited Walton Bury[16], the home of Mrs Allsopp and her only daughter, Cynthia. Cynthia's father, Captain Herbert Tongue Allsopp was the 5th son of the 1st Baron Hindlip of Hindlip Hall, Worcester. He had suffered a mental breakdown at the outbreak of war, was in a nursing home and not expected to return to Walton. Sir Arthur had heard that the Allsopps' had a very extensive cellar and that maybe he could perhaps purchase wine for special occasions!

The Earl of Lichfield (1856–1918)

He also visited the Earl of Shrewsbury at Ingestre, and Shugborough Hall, the home of the Earl of Lichfield. He described Shugborough Park as very beautiful but the house as ugly. However, he did admire the furniture and Chinese curios that the Earl showed him. It was the Earl of Lichfield who had permitted the War Office to construct the camps on Cannock Chase. The Earl died on 29th July, 1918. He was found shot through the head on the banks of the river near the Hall. The Inquest held the following day at Shugborough recorded a verdict of "Accidental Death".

[16] Now converted to apartments and known as Oakover Grange.

The Doctor suggested that he had slipped on mossy ground and somehow discharged his loaded gun.

Sir Arthur was keen to make the acquaintance of the new Earl and he visited Shugborough early in October to join a shoot. He and his two dogs, Raggie and Lassie, who always accompanied him, were familiar figures at many of the local shoots, including Milford, Ingestre, Tixall and Teddesley. And of course he found time to see his family who were now living in Brocton.

Lassie gave birth to pups and Sir Arthur presented one to Dyonése Levett. Her dog was called Don, perhaps after the river that flowed past the House of Monymusk in Aberdeenshire. Don would be a faithful companion to Dyonése for many years.

Chapter 4

The Camp

The Camp was situated on the top of Cannock Chase, over 600 feet above sea level and about 5 miles from Stafford - the nearest town of any size. In summer it appeared to be an idyllic place, gently undulating land covered in heather, bracken, bilberries and blackberries, with ancient oaks and pines towering above the nearby villages of Milford and Brocton. However, in winter, it was a very different story. The wind blew straight from the Welsh Hills cutting through the worn and shabby uniforms of the Prisoners of War, chilling them to the bone. Often there was snow covering the camp when none could be found in the surrounding villages just half a mile away.

The Prisoners were housed in standard wooden huts (60ft x 20ft) raised up off the ground and lined with Poilite[17] as a means of insulation, with a door at each end. There was a stove in the middle for warmth, and twelve windows letting in the light. The three electric light bulbs that hung from the ceiling did little to brighten such a large space in the long dark days of winter. Two windows, one at each end of the hut, were (or should have been) kept permanently open for ventilation. Cerebro-spinal meningitis, caused either by a virus or bacterial infection, was known to spread through the huts if ventilation was inadequate. A constant battle raged between the Commandant and the prisoners, in an effort to either open or close the windows. The Commandant would eventually win this battle! Each hut

[17] A form of Asbestos sheeting used in buildings

could provide, at a push, accommodation for up to a maximum of 40 men.

The Camp was divided into sections, each with thirty-six barrack huts surrounding a Cook House, Drying Room, Bath House and an Ablutions Hut. With room for forty prisoners in each hut, there could be up to 1,440 prisoners in a section.

"C" Line however was a little different, as this was the Prisoners' Hospital under the control, when first opened, of Lt. Colonel Michael O'Halloran. O'Halloran had served in India and then in South Africa from 1899 until 1902, the same time as the Commandant was fighting the Boers; perhaps they were old acquaintances. Second in command in the Hospital was Sub-Commander Harold Hebblethwaite, aided by two operating surgeons and several other doctors. While Harold Hebblethwaite was working to save the lives of German soldiers, his son Arthur, also a doctor, was risking his own life training stretcher bearers and supervising them under fire at The Front.

O'Halloran was a difficult man to deal with and it was not long before Sir Arthur found it necessary to hint to the General that all was not well in the Hospital. He had found, on two consecutive days, an officer drunk on duty. The two men had also had a disagreement over 6/6d which was due to be paid for breakages in the Hospital. After 30 memos, Sir Arthur proved his point, but their relationship was never going to be easy and they quarrelled regularly. By July things were even worse. General Davies sent for O'Halloran, Hebblethwaite and Sir Arthur and O'Halloran subsequently received a very severe dressing down for allowing women into the Camp!

Colonel O'Halloran had presented a completely different facet of his personality when the hospital was inspected by the Swiss Legation on 20th June, 1917. The report says that "he was a broad-minded man, an extremely able hospital superintendent and in the name of all his patients we wish to thank him."[18]

In June, Sir W. Essex, M.P. for Stafford raise the question, in the House of Commons, as to whether a German doctor by the name of Staab had been or was to be sent to assists the prisoners at Brocton. He was informed that no German doctor had been or was to be sent to Brocton Camp.[19]

In the Hospital, five large huts contained 36 beds but the remaining 36 huts had just 22 beds. The Isolation Ward had 25 beds and the Ward for serious cases was subdivided into semi-private accommodation. This had facilities for just twenty patients. One ward was set aside for officers and was partitioned into single rooms. Each ward had its own bathroom, w.c. and a small isolation room. There was an Operating Theatre and Receiving Rooms for both stretcher cases and the walking wounded.

The hospital food was better than that of the other prisoners and some patients received special diets to help them recover from their injuries or illness. The kitchen was run by a R.A.M.C. sergeant, assisted by 8 German prisoners. Although there was a large dining room most of the patients were unable to leave their beds and so their food was delivered by means of hand-pushed dinner wagons.

---

[18] WO 383-432

[19] Hansard 27th June 1917

Convalescing prisoners were recruited to help with such duties within the hospital. Within two months of the Camp opening, the Hospital had 639 patients but, by the end of 1918, it was considered necessary to incorporate "B" lines into the hospital to cope with the ever increasing number of injured men.

The perimeter of the camp was defined by a belt of tangled barbed wire some 6ft wide, whilst a line of plain wire fastened to white posts on the inside marked the point beyond which PoWs were not allowed to go. The area between the two barriers was known by the prisoners as the "Death Run" and any PoW entering it could be shot at by a sentry after one challenge. Marking the outer boundary of the barbed wire entanglement was a tall wire fence, some 10 ft high, with an overhang inward of 3 wires fixed on arms nailed to the high posts. Every 300 yards or so there was a lookout tower where a sentry kept watch for any attempts to escape through the wire.

Sir Arthur was concerned as to the security of the Camp as, on two sides, the wire ran practically at the doors of the huts. Within 2 yards of it on one side were quartered the R.A.M.C[20] & R.D.C[21]. The other side was earmarked for the arrival of New Zealand troops in September. He had advised that a space of at least 30 ft, both within and without the wire, should always be left clear of buildings in order to

[20] R.A.M.C. Royal Army Medical Corps.

[21] R.D.C. Royal Defence Corps The role of the regiment was to provide troops for security and guard duties inside the UK guarding important locations such as ports or bridges. It also provided independent companies for guarding PoW Camps. The regiment was never intended to be employed on overseas service.

enable the sentries to see clearly, to prevent illicit communication and to prevent tunnelling.

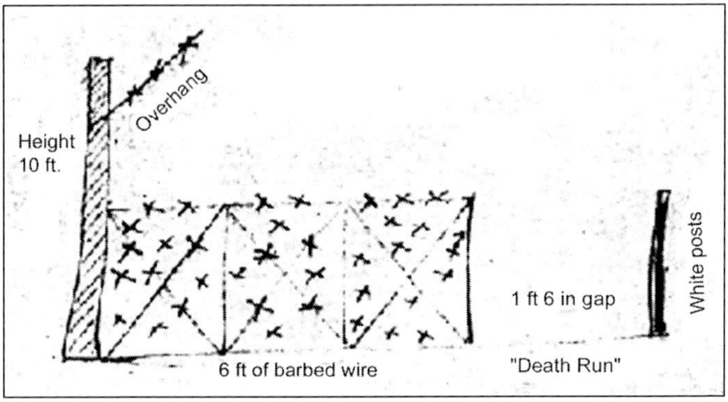

Diagram of Barrier surrounding the PoW Camp

As the lines occupied by the prisoners had originally been built to house the 1st and 2nd Infantry Brigades, there had been no need to leave space between the various groups of huts and from time to time, disagreements arose between the prisoners and the New Zealanders who resided within shouting distance of them. The Kiwis considered that the Germans spent a lazy internment behind barbed wire - well fed, underworked, splendidly housed, and sometimes insolent. It is reported that the New Zealand troops regularly took pleasure in annoying the prisoners by throwing stones onto the tin roofs of their huts!

Although many of the prisoners had been injured, and several were amputees, it was important to keep as many people as possible "busy". Some were detailed for cleaning and keeping everything in good order, although the prisoners were found not to be too particular when it came to the care of the latrines and bath houses! Although some prisoners complained about the standard of their accommodation, all the huts were of exactly the same design as those provided for the British and New Zealand troops.

Washing and cooking kept other groups busy. The cooks were distinguished by their white uniform worn over their regular clothes. The quality of food was excellent, although some prisoners were prone to complain at any opportunity. It was possible, if funds and provisions allowed, for prisoners to supplement their diet by purchasing commodities from the canteen. Others were kept busy both in and outside of the camp.

A World War 1 Hut

Sir Arthur had proved that he could command respect both from his staff and the prisoners and he soon received several visits from "high up" officers inspecting the Camp. Everyone seemed pleased with the way things were being run and on 20th June 1917, Sir Arthur heard that he was to have another twenty camps under his command.

Chapter 5

Keeping Everyone Busy

Sir Arthur's first task on arrival was to get control of the camp and of the prisoners. Immediately he set the PoWs to work clearing the paths and the parade ground. Daily inspections ensured that the huts themselves, and the prisoners, were clean and tidy. The Commandant even instigated a weekly prize for the best hut.

Box made by Prisoner Otto Fischer for the Commandant [22]

[22] The Box is engraved with the words "Suum Cuique", a Latin phrase that translates into English as "to each his own". It was the motto of the Order of the Black Eagle, the highest order of chivalry in Prussia during the time of Frederick the Great. (1740 – 1786) It is also the motto of the Faculty of Advocates in Scotland.

Within a month, the Camp was looking presentable and the prisoners had received a selection of flower and vegetable seeds which they were eager to sow. Rhododendrons were also planted between the huts. A garden was developed around the Commandant's quarters and an arbour, covered with heather was built in front of it. As it was so windy, there was some concern as to how the arbour would withstand the weather! The inside of his bungalow was painted by a prisoner and eventually some of the prisoners' huts were also painted.

April had been particularly dry and there was fear of a bad heath fire. A large group of prisoners were set to cut down extensive areas of heather & bracken around the camp in case a fire should start. The bracken was sold to the Potteries for packing drain pipes!

Building a road around the Camp was a project used as punishment for prisoners who were reluctant to work. The construction was slow and hard, at least until the road reached the flat area of the Chase. It had been nick- named the "Via Dolorosa", the "Way of Grief", and by the end of October it was possible to drive all-round the camp in a motor car.

Some prisoners continued working at the trades they had known before the war, and a number of shops flourished within the Camp. Everyone was expected to maintain certain standards and therefore there was a need for a regular visit to the Barber's Shop. Wounded and needy prisoners were not charged, but those who worked had to pay the going rate. Even the Commandant made use of this service. He was so pleased with his hair cut that he gave the barber a shilling rather than the 1d he had requested

By September a trained dentist tried, with limited equipment, to keep the Prisoners' teeth healthy and free from pain. Again a small charge was made for those who could afford to pay.

The Tailors' shop was incredibly busy. The prisoners' uniforms were often cast-off British ones which had been dyed. Very rarely did they fit and it was the job of the tailors to remake the garments and finally complete the outfits by embellishing them with large blue or red circular patches so that, should a chap escape, he would soon be spotted by local residents or the police.

The Newspapers have arrived

Whenever a prisoner feared there was something amiss with his watch, he would visit the watchmaker. As well as undertaking repairs for prisoners, who were always anxious to keep an eye on the time, the watchmaker also took in work from a Stafford jeweller. Some local people may have been a little upset to discover their precious timepiece had been overhauled by a Hun.

Up to thirteen shoemakers were employed in the Cobbler's shop, and they struggled to cope with all the work. The boots supplied for prisoners were usually partly worn, and it was not long before they were in need of repair. Not only were the Cobblers responsible for the footwear of the several thousand prisoners at Brocton, but they were also required to repair boots from other nearby smaller camps and the working camps under Brocton's command.

A Printer's Shop provided a daily "Newspaper" in German. The Prisoners were allowed copies of both English and French newspapers, but many men could only read German and so the camp newspaper "Deutsche Zeitung Broctonlager"[23] was a vital link to keep them in touch with the outside world. The printers also produced programmes for theatrical or musical performances, of which there were many. They also ran a book binding service to help keep the many much-read volumes in the Camp library in reasonable condition.

There were two Carpenter's Shops; one was responsible for all the repair work around the camp as well as work on damaged furniture. The other was of a more specialist nature, creating intricate and inventive work which was

[23] Translates, as "German Newspaper Brocton Camp!"

often sold outside the camp. Sometimes exhibitions of Prisoners' work were held for the local community.

Being kept busy!

All the fit PoWs had work of some kind, but Sir Arthur expected trouble as, to start with, they were being paid just one halfpenny per hour. After expressing his concerns, he was given permission, after just a month, to increase their pay to 1d per hour..

In 1917 a 33 year old Jew, Arnold Zadikow, who had originally been totally opposed to war but had eventually been persuaded to join the Cavalry, arrived at Brocton Camp. He had been severely injured in the back and was destined to spend the rest of the War in Brocton. Arnold began his working career as a stone mason before becoming a master builder. He soon turned his talents to creative

work, making many small plaques in metal as well as larger sculptures. Whilst in Brocton he was provided with materials to enable him to continue working.

We know of one plaster cast made by Arnold which is now in the British Museum. On the reverse is the dedication "Out of the Barbed Wire. To Staff Sergeant Edwards by Arnold Zadikow, Munich, P/W Brocton." Many other bronze medals depicting war and death, made before his capture, still survive.

In April 1919, as his time at Brocton was coming to an end, Arnold[24] designed a small bronze statue of a man half-kneeling and looking to the future, as a permanent memorial to all the prisoners of war who had died whilst at Brocton. The statue, just twelve inches high was made by A.B. Burton of Thames Ditton, one of the leading Bronze founders in Britain who were responsible for casting many famous war memorials through-

[24] In the Second World War, Zadikow died in the Theresienstadt Concentration Camp.

out the country. Mounted on a wooden block into which are carved the words "Furs Vaterland" and the date 1918, it is now in the possession of Sir Arthur's grandson.

Out of the Barbed Wire

The Commandant was aware that many of the men were under-employed. He had seen five men mending lights – but two men and sometimes four of the men, were doing nothing, apart from watching, all the time! As well as working in the Camp, parties of five or six prisoners together with two guards would undertake work in the surrounding area. They would go to local farms or help elderly people maintain their gardens, as well as working on larger projects such as constructing the concrete lining to Oldacre Brook close to the Camp,[25] under the supervision of the Royal Engineers.

Nearly every farm within three miles of the camp had prisoners working in the fields, planting potatoes, picking peas, cutting thistles or any other job that the farmer needed doing. At one time, over a hundred such gangs set out each morning from Brocton.

In 1917, a Director of Timber Supplies was appointed. His duties were to control the supply of timber for the Army, and effect economies in its use in the United Kingdom whilst stimulating its production. The yard of local timber company, Henry Venables of Doxey, was commandeered as a storage depot for several mills.

Trusted prisoners travelled by train from Milford to Stafford each day to help unload trains bringing timber to the yard, where it was stacked, cut and dried. Then, when required, they loaded it on to a train or truck for delivery in accordance with the Army's instructions.

[25] Information provided by Margaret Smallwood in 1992

Henry Venables Saw Mill

Most prisoners worked an eight hour day in summer, and a seven hour day in winter, for 1d an hour. Travelling time to and from work was not included in their working hours. Saturday afternoon was free, and all workers received extra rations. The camp cobblers, tailors and the camp leader were the lucky ones, and more affluent than most. They received one and a half pence per hour!

Lt. Boulger, one of the interpreters, ran what amounted to a small bank in which Prisoners could save their meagre earnings, or deposit money sent to them from relatives and friends in Germany. Occasionally there were gifts of money from the Red Cross. Privates were allowed to withdraw up to 10/- weekly from their credit, and NCO's able to withdraw up to £1.

By the Spring of 1918, the demand for Prisoner labour in farming areas increased drastically. To meet it, Agricultural Depots were formed in various parts of the country, nine of them being opened under Brocton.[26] As well as Agricultural Depots there were many smaller Agricultural Camps under Brocton's control, mainly in the rural parts of Lincolnshire, Leicestershire and Nottinghamshire. Farmers employing Prisoners of War were required to fetch them from camp and return them no later than half an hour after sunset each evening. The prisoners were not allowed to walk more than three miles to their place of work, so farmers had to provide transport if the men were required to work further afield. Food for the prisoners was provided by the military authorities.[27]

Exploring his far flung camps, Sir Arthur visited a small camp in the Fens. The land was the most wonderful farming land he had ever seen and he claimed that it was making a fortune for the farmers. They all seemed to own motors and were sending their sons away to university. They were becoming the new gentry!

Just how difficult it was to run a farm became clear when Lord Shrewsbury's agent explained that, in normal times, he had 100 men to look after 35,000 acres. Now he was relying on a few workers too old to fight and the PoWs.

Many local farmers were keen to ask for assistance. In April, 1918, four men were sent to help at Barnfields Farm. Mr Edwards at Stockton Farm, Walton, requested 3 men - 2 to milk and 1 for field work and old Mrs Holt of Milford

[26] A list of Agriculatural Depots & Camps under Brocton's control can be found in the Appendix.

[27] Grantham Journal 10th August 1918

wanted 1 milker and 2 to work the horses. Two PoWs worked for Thomas Fallows on the farm at Shugborough. They had the luxury of lodging at the farm and did not have to return to Camp each night[28]. It meant that they were on hand to start work bright and early. Prisoners were also sent to work, under armed guard, in the gardens at Hatherton, Milford and Shugborough Hall. The prisoners who worked at Milford Hall made regular use of the pool for their ablutions. Although the water was cold it was better than waiting your turn at the Camp!

William Mynors began to employ German prisoners at Ingestre in April 1918. Their first task was to cut shrubs and empty the sewage tanks. Prisoners continued to work in the gardens but on 10th September their work was found to be "untidily done" and William had, at the end of the day, to straighten up their efforts! Perhaps they were happier painting the greenhouse, a task undertaken on 19th September. Before long 120 Germans were working on farms, gardens and estates in the area.

The farmers were impressed with the speed Sir Arthur dealt with their requests for help. Previously it had been a question of forms and delay, then delay and more forms! Under Sir Arthur help was received within days.

Sir Arthur travelled widely to visit the other camps under his control and to check on the working parties. Locally, prisoners were digging gravel, but further afield near Catterick, they were quarrying ganister[29], which was used in the

[28] Working under Scheme B See Page 135

[29] a close-grained, hard siliceous rock found in the coal measures of northern England..

manufacture of fireproof brick for furnaces. Not far from Catterick other prisoners were working in the quarries helping to meet the requirement for 120,000 tons of limestone per week. His exploration of other camps was cut short at the end of July when he was unable to obtain any petrol! When available again it had risen in price to 4/3d per gallon.[30]

By June 1917 Sir Arthur reported that he had four thousand and nine prisoners in his care at Brocton, including four hundred and seventy eight in the camp hospital.

30 Petrol was only at this price for a relatively short period, but in 1960 it was still only 4/9d per gallon!

Chapter 6

All in a Days Work – 1917

Sir Arthur had been at Brocton less than a fortnight before he had a message to say 1500 more Huns would be arriving within the week. The camp was by no means ready and there was frantic action to try and make everything ship-shape.

The prisoners arrived from France; all were dirty and most were lousy. Captured on 9th April they seemed to have had enough of war. They brought with them large quantities of food, which was confiscated to be used as a standby when rations were low. Their pockets were stuffed with biscuits which they were allowed to keep - nobody in their right minds would want to eat them! They were not allowed their knives, folks and spoons; these would be re-issued in due course. They also carried a large quantity of field dressings and compresses; the Hospital would find them very useful.

By September the lines were completely full and so a party of Swiss and English doctors arrived to examine the PoWs to select some who would be repatriated or sent to Holland or Switzerland. Some of the prisoners were really ill but others were shamming, prepared to get up to all sorts of dodges in an effort to be passed for Switzerland. Some starved themselves so that they appeared faint; others took large quantities of aspirin, all in a desperate bid to get away. It was reported that one man, not at Brocton, had eaten a box of match heads in an attempt to appear ill and very nearly died!

Eventually 1000 men were selected to go to Switzerland, they were put into "E" & "F" lines, the "workers" were put in "B" lines and the "drones" in "A" lines, thus preventing any workers being able to hide away and escape their duties. Throughout the life of the Camp it was the "A" lines that caused the least trouble. Once this batch of 1000 prisoners had departed via Dorchester, a large amount of soap was found to be missing. At least they would be clean!

The departing prisoners were replaced on 14th October by a train load of severely wounded prisoners, who were carried from the train to awaiting Red Cross motor ambulances, on stretchers.[31] About a dozen people had gathered to see what was happening including William Mynors and young Laura Dutton who was visiting a friend who lived in the railway cottages.

Brocton Camp contained a nucleus of prisoners of dubious character who needed very little encouragement to cause trouble and on two occasions, to start a strike. The "bad apples", it seemed, were all in "B" lines, and this is where the trouble always started.

In October 1917 the temperature dropped. The coal ration, which was issued each day at 9 a.m., was consumed before nightfall. As always, there are two sides to every story and the prisoners were quick to complain that no coal was

[31] Extract from the Diary of William Mynors

available next morning for the kitchen to cook their breakfast.

Prisoners at Brocton

A delegation of prisoners complained that "Working parties were expected to walk several miles to their place of work, and slave away all day without any nourishment. They were not prepared to work in such circumstances." A shot from the Commandant's gun, close to one of the prisoners, made them all move and they were soon back at work.

That there was no coal was the fault of the prisoners themselves. The coal ration was issued each morning and had to last for 24 hours. If coal had been stolen, which happened regularly, a reduced amount was issued to make up the deficiency. After his repatriation, Ernest Ornen wrote to his friend about their coal ration. "The time passed very slowly in Brocton as it was very cold. We only left our beds when paraded. We received 1 scuttle of coals in 3 days and this was only sufficient for one (day). However, we knew what to do and we stole lots of coal in spite of the sentry who was always posted outside the coal stores. One of us engaged the sentry in conversation while the others robbed the coal stores properly".

On the occasion of the first strike, the full ration had been issued but the prisoners had chosen to use it all during the day, leaving nothing with which to cook breakfast.

To supplement the coal ration, prisoners had been allowed to bring in a large amount of dead wood from the surrounding area to burn on their stoves. Against all orders, a day or two earlier the prisoners had brought back green wood and, as a consequence, the privilege of bringing firewood into Camp was withdrawn.

On 1st November very few working parties went out. It appeared that suddenly there were a large number of Roman Catholic prisoners who wished to mark All Saints Day. Was this a sudden conversion on the part of many?

The Commandant decided on a regular basis, to patrol the camp, well after lights out. He found huts with all the windows closed and quickly roused the sleeping Germans and sent them outside. Having to leave their beds during the night was as a result of the prisoners' failure to keep two windows open to prevent the build-up of foul air. They were only out of their huts for about five minutes while the ventilation improved, and then they were allowed to return - as long as the windows remained open! Pity the poor prisoner who had to sleep under an open window whatever the weather! All prisoners were well aware that they would be told to vacate the hut if they failed to obey the instructions and leave the window open. After spending time outside they realised that the Commandant meant what he said. The lesson was learnt, until a new batch of prisoners arrived and the process had to be gone through again!

On Christmas Eve, 1917, Birley and Sir Arthur travelled into Stafford and bought coloured paper to allow the prisoners to make streamers for their huts and in the evening the men in "prison" were released as a gesture of good will but, as Sir Arthur returned to his quarters, he found two men stealing coal yet again. They ran away and were not caught; so, as punishment, the theatre was closed and all coals to the huts stopped, The gate between the 2 lines was also closed. Not a Happy Christmas!

The second strike took place on 27th December, 1917. Started again by "B" lines, pressure was put on the more law abiding residents of "A" lines who eventually, rather reluctantly, joined in. The prisoners were due to return to work after the Christmas break but they refused. Although no reason for the strike was given, it was assumed that, after having extra rations during the holiday they felt they would like to extend their break rather than be involved in manual labour.

The Commandant was informed of the strike and there was some concern as to whether a serious disturbance had been planned and was imminent. When Sir Arthur arrived at the Parade Ground where the prisoners had been drawn up, he became aware that some prisoners were behaving in an insolent and defiant manner. He opened his shot gun to show the men that it was loaded but one prisoner placed himself immediately in front of him and adopted a violent and aggressive attitude. Sir Arthur sent him flying and the prisoner was arrested. The Commandant feared he might have to shoot one of the ringleaders. The trouble necessitated a display of force, and the New Zealanders from the nearby huts were ordered out under arms, and machine-guns were placed in position covering the prison camp enclosure. Another troublesome individual was arrested and the prisoners eventually realised that the Commandant was not to be trifled with.

The strike began at 8 a.m. and lasted until 4 p.m. The prisoners were kept on parade until their conduct became normal. From time to time parties were marched off to the latrines but, in spite of this, some sixteen prisoners found it necessary to relieve themselves where they stood. They were immediately confined until the evening, their actions being construed as a further attempt to disrupt Camp discipline.

Then there was a complaint that, whilst they were kept on parade, the guards had robbed their huts. This was completely untrue and no prisoner could name any item that had gone missing from their belongings.

Sir Arthur was keen to show the prisoners that he was in charge and that they should obey his commands. Behaviour was much improved after this event, but it was noted that yet again, the ring leaders were prisoners in "B" lines.

Sir Arthur had his own complaint! It was that the only punishment allowed for Non Commissioned Officers was to stop their letters and parcels for one month.

He commented that, as many did not get any letters, they only laughed at such a pitiful sentence. At the end of the month all letter and parcels were to be given to the culprits. Letters came to no harm, but parcels containing food stuffs would perhaps be a little smelly! As it was not unusual for parcels to take months to arrive the Commandant could hardly be blamed when things were past their best!

More German Prisoners (The Theatre Group) including 2 German Imperial Navy Sailors.

"All is fair in love and war", or so they say, but is it fair to steal from your comrades? The German Camp Leader, Knetch, reported that he had caught 2 men stealing their companion's parcels. They were immediately put in the Guard Room to be dealt with in due course. A few days later, the Canteen in "E" & "F" lines was broken into and goods worth over £5 had been stolen. Two prisoners were each given a month in "prison", one for stealing a blanket and the other for cutting the wire between the two enclosures.

As prisoners left, others arrived, and all had to be searched to ensure that they did not have anything which could help them escape. These searches uncovered some unusual items! One prisoner from the Cameroons[32] still had all his kit; he also had a quiver full of arrows! How he managed to bring them as far as Brocton is difficult to explain. This fellow told tales of meeting an ex-cannibal, who had informed him that the most delicious part of a human being was the left arm of a baby! There was nothing unusual about finding knives and field glasses, or small items of jewellery, lace and silk, things which were always confiscated, but how did one prisoner come complete with a beautiful fur coat? Another had an Edward 1 silver coin which was seized to prevent it being exported to Germany.

As the temperature dropped, a count was done of the blankets in the stores. There were over a hundred missing. Sir Arthur was sure many would turn up, most likely on the beds of the prisoners, but he did wonder how many had gone away in the bags of prisoners leaving the camp, and what had the Quarter Master been doing to allow such a discrepancy?

[32] The Germans were able to recruit an army of 6,000 men from their colony in Cameroon

Chapter 7

Family Life

Evie Grant was devoted to her husband. She had nursed him back to health from the injuries he sustained at the Front in 1915, so, when he was declared fit for service on the home front, she missed him terribly. The couple exchanged letters daily and on hearing of Arthur's appointment as Commandant, she wrote to ask "Where is Brocton?"

A few days later she put pen to paper again, suggesting that they should try and rent a house for the family whereby they could at least be near to one another but, she needed to know exactly where on the Chase the camp was situated as "the Chase is so big!"

Within three days there was news that Mrs Chetwynd was to let Brocton Hall for eight and a half guineas[33] per week, with gardener and all produce thrown in. There was no time to waste as many officers were trying to find homes in the area for their families. Evie came dashing to Staffordshire and after she and her husband had visited Brocton Hall, she contacted the agents, Evans & Evans, to offer a rent of seven and a half guineas a week on condition that the water and drains were tested and found to be satisfactory. Brocton Hall had obviously been a very splendid house in the past, but now it had a rather neglected air and was not as clean as Evie would have liked. Although supposedly furnished, it lacked the most basic of equipment

[33] Guinea equals One Pound and one shilling.

but there was a large, rather regal bed! The rooms were lit by oil lamps and heated by coal fires but it would do for the summer. Sir Arthur signed the lease on 16th May.

Mrs Mary Chetwynd, now 56, had been widowed in 1895. Her only son had married at 20, the 17 year old daughter of a brewery drayman, a girl of whom she did not approve. It was a marriage not destined to last. Earlier in the year there had been some unpleasantness when Mrs Chetwynd junior had been found in bed with her husband's friend while they were all guests at the Hall!

Beatrice, Mary's eldest daughter, was working at the General Lying-in Hospital in London and Mildred, the youngest of her three children, was never in paid employment. She spent her time doing charity work. The girls were making lives for themselves and Mary thought she would enjoy spending time with them in London, away from the gossips. The time was right for a move from Brocton.[34] She was the daughter of George Meakin, the earthenware manufacturer, and the family owned several other houses, including Cresswell Hall,[35] north of Stafford, so she would not be short of a home. She accepted the offer of rent made by Sir Arthur, on condition that he paid to have the water and drains tested.

Evie was anxious to get things moving as she was expecting their fifth child in August. On 11th May she reported that the analysis of the water had indicated that it

[34] Although she returned to Brocton Hall after the Grant's had moved to Brocton Leys, the Hall was put up for auction in 1920 and eventually sold to the Golf Club..

[35] Demolished 1938

was safe to live by, but the children must not paddle in it! Some work was necessary on the drains but they would definitely take the house immediately and sort the drains out in due course. By the 20th May the family had moved to Brocton Hall and Evie contacted Mrs Chetwynd to ask about trades people in the area, particularly the coal agent, as such a large house would take some heating.[36]

Once the family were living at Brocton Hall, Sir Arthur would often come down from Camp to fish in the pond or shoot rooks and snipe. He decided to explore the whole of the house, as there were several rooms and out-buildings he had not investigated prior to signing the lease. He discovered that every loft and attic was filled with rubbish of every kind and covered with dust and dirt.

Brocton Hall

[36] Mr W, Smallwood of Brocton Village was the coal agent.

Although Sir Arthur was just over a mile away when he was on duty, Evie still wrote to him regularly. Having a husband in charge of several thousand men had its advantages. On 9th July she wrote "May we have some Germans down here tomorrow, Tuesday. The black-currants are all ready for jam and I'd like to get them picked as soon as possible before the birds get them. And can you buy me as much sugar from the canteen as you can.

Mrs Lascelles[37] told me that if we bought from other stores as well, the canteen would let us have 7lbs of sugar with each order."

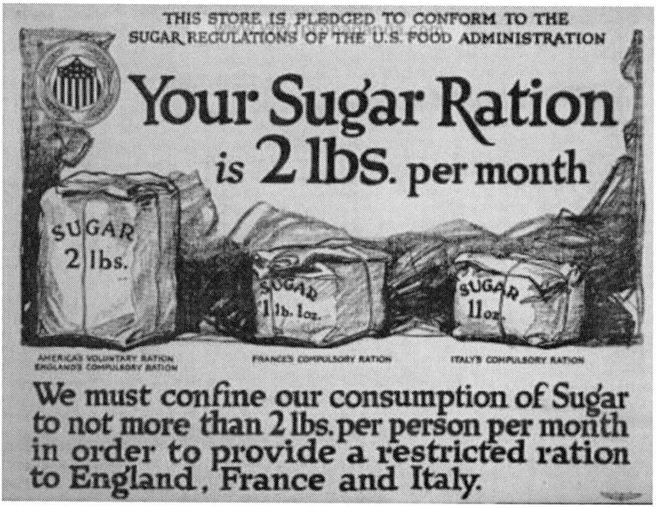

Just before Christmas, Sir Arthur received from his mother, who was living in London, a consignment of sugar that had been "rescued" from a sugar factory which had

[37] Wife of Col. Edward F.W. Lascelles, a New Zealander who have served in South Africa & India at the same time as Sir Arthur.

been completely destroyed by fire! Too late for jam making, but it would help supplement the family's rations.

Although happy to make use of German labour in the garden, Evie had strong feelings about them working on her husband's car which had recently arrived in Brocton. She wrote to him saying, "I am glad that the car has come alright – but please don't on any account allow a Hun to look after it – not one of them is to be trusted and there are so many things that can be done to the machinery or any part of the car, to cause an accident"[38]

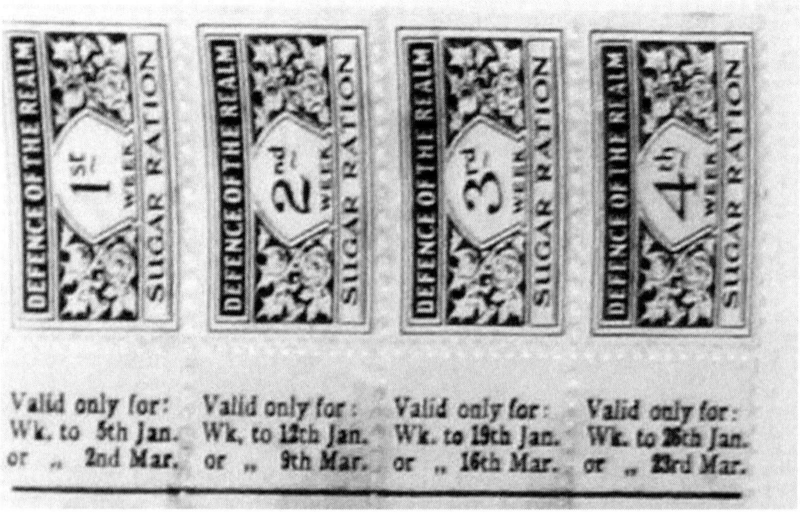

Sugar Ration Coupons

Her husband did not heed her warning as he employed a German sailor named Trangis, with experience of marine engines, as his mechanic. Sir Arthur had nothing but praise for this man and he allowed him to completely strip down the engine and do any necessary repairs.

[38] GD 345/1433 National Records of Scotland

Lady Grant with Evelyn (7), Arthur (6), Elspeth (4), Francis (3) and Jean at 2 months in 1917

Reproduced by courtesy of Sir Archibald & Lady Fiona Grant

The family soon settled down to life in Brocton. The two eldest children, Evelyn and young Arthur, (who was always referred to as Podge by everyone, except his father) were allowed to help with the hay making on Milford Hall Estate, and the family regularly attended the local Church. There were also exciting trips in the car exploring the surrounding countryside. On 18th August Evie gave birth to a daughter, Catherine Jean, at Brocton Hall and on the 22nd September the new baby was christened at the village church in Walton on the Hill.

Everything was fine during the summer but, as winter approached, Evie realised that the large rooms with high ceilings would be impossible to keep warm when it was so hard to obtain coal. It was not a place to bring up a new baby and they certainly did not need ten bedrooms when it was almost impossible to get staff. The children were constantly ill with colds and the house, built early in the 19th century, was draughty and in need of constant maintenance. Then there was the story of the house being haunted. Young Arthur claimed to have seen something "spooky" that looked like a white owl and there were also stories in the village of a ghost!

November 1917 saw the family move to Brocton Leys. Built in 1900 it offered modern conveniences, a large garden, was not as large or as isolated as the Hall, and was even nearer to the Camp than Brocton Hall.

It was just a gentle downhill walk of ten minutes from Sir Arthur's quarters to his family in the Village. However, things did not run smoothly! After a couple of days the cook informed Evie that she was going, as she could not possibly live in such a small place where she had to eat in the kitchen! Cook did not leave immediately, but her next complaint was not long in coming. She did not like the fact that the family were abiding by the food restrictions imposed by the Government and claimed that she could easily get a job with a family where there was plenty of food!

Brocton Leys

Reproduced by courtesy of Mr C. Phillips

Although it was important, because of Sir Arthur's position, that the family obeyed the government restrictions, things were not that bad. After a trip to Ingestre or Hatherton Hall, visits he made regularly, Sir Arthur would return with peaches or a lovely bunch of grapes and he had apples sent from Monymusk. Sometimes a 10 lb salmon would arrive from the Scottish estate. He would also come home with trout, pheasants or a rabbit or two caught or shot on one of his many days out. He would often combine a visit to check on working parties with a little shooting alongside the farmer or landowner.

Then, in the New Year, the children's governess left without giving notice but it would appear that she was not missed!

After spending over £12 on various repairs to Brocton Hall, and paying a reasonable rent, Sir Arthur was more than a little surprised to receive at the start of the year, a bill for damages from Mrs Chetwynd! Among the many petty and vexatious charges, she was claiming 1/6d for a handle off a frying pan! This had already been broken before the family had put a foot into Brocton Hall. Despite these problems, the family continued to enjoy life in Brocton. Gifts for their first Christmas in Staffordshire came from the prisoners' workshops. There was a little wooden clown and a swinging parrot for Arthur, a nice box for Evie, (costing Sir Arthur 25/3d) and a cigarette case, complete with the family crest for Sir Arthur. There was also a splendid turkey sent from Scotland.

There was often afternoon tea or more formal dinners with Captain & Mrs Levett at Milford Hall, Mrs Allsopp at Walton Bury or Mr & Mrs Joy[39] at the White Lodge, Milford. A couple of New Zealand officers were sometimes recruited to join the regular tennis parties at Walton Bury. There were also many outings in the car to all parts of the county accompanying Sir Arthur when he was inspecting working parties. Although they no longer lived at Brocton Hall, the whole family would skate there when the pond was frozen. They also had a German prisoner as their full-time gardener who grew vegetables and who did not let the flowers die as the Brocton Hall gardener had done.

[39] Mr Joy was Clerk to the County Council

Chapter 8

A Day in Camp

A shrill whistle shatters my dreams - slowly I open my eyes. It is dark outside and the never ending rain is battering down on the roof of our hut. As the electric lights in the hut give out a dim light, I see several of my companions struggling to get out from under their blankets, for any minute now the coffee buckets will arrive, collected by some restless fellow prisoner eager to be first in the queue at the Cook House. It is half past six and still very dark.

German Prisoners in their Hut

Forty wooden mugs set out the previous evening are arranged in a row, and each is filled with warm coffee. It had been hot when it left the Cook House but the morning is cold and the walk through the pouring rain does little to preserve the temperature of our first drink of the day.

Then there is the rush to the corrugated–iron wash house, I drape my towel over my head and shoulder as protection against the weather. I grab one of the six washing bowls and then wait patiently for my turn to fill it with water from one of the two taps. There is no time to waste as already, others are demanding that you hurry with the washing bowls and "please don't take too much water" as it has to go round almost three hundred people. Ablutions finished, I return to the hut for breakfast.

My bread ration is carefully cut in two. One half is for breakfast, the other half put on one side for later. We are allocated margarine twice a week so, if I have been careful, there may be some left to put on my bread - otherwise it will just be dry bread with my coffee.

Some comrades have breakfast in bed, choosing to get up in a leisurely manner. A discussion rages as to whether the working parties will be going out today because the weather conditions are appalling. About half of those in our hut are employed on local farms or working with the Royal Engineers on construction projects. I am not yet fit enough to join a working party, so I do not have to worry too much about the rain.

We are all summoned by a whistle, to be counted – a performance that happens twice a day, usually around 7.30 a.m and 4.00 p.m. depending on the time of year and the time all the working parties have returned to camp. It is no use, we have to go out in the rain and trudge along the wet paths to the parade ground. By half past seven a grey dawn hangs over the countryside, crisscrossed by long rows of lamps along the barbed wire fence. It is now a frantic rush for all those who had decided to take things easy and stay in bed!

Gradually, members of each hut line up in fours, standing in the squelchy mud and trying our best to avoid the larger puddles. Eventually, the man standing nearest the puddles must, whether he likes it or not, stand in them. The work details line up to one side in a never ending column of groups. Still it rains, and I can feel the cold seeping into my bones and I realise that my boots are no longer water-tight. It will be another fortnight before our boots are inspected, and then I will be able to have mine repaired.

Another shrill whistle and a bugle call followed by the order "Attention – Eyes left.". The Officer in Charge appears and the roll is taken. Another word of command: "Eyes Front" and at the same time "Forty, Sir". Two English sergeants run back and forth counting to make sure no-one has escaped during the night, or is still in bed! To make the count easier, 40 men are supposed to stand in each row, and in the background the numbers are being added up.It takes so long, the men step restlessly from one leg to another. Finally it emerges that there are two men too many in one row. The count starts again, and thank goodness there were only 38 in another row. The count is correct. The rain has eased and I can return to my hut whilst the working parties march off to toil under the watchful eyes of their sergeants.

While some take off their wet boots and return shivering, to their beds in an effort to get warm again, I head for the only comfortable room in the camp - the reading room at the back of the theatre. Separated from the main body of the theatre by bits of stage scenery, I come first to the Barber's Shop where two barbers, dressed in white, huddle

Time to be counted

round the stove warming their hands before they commence their days' work. The first customers are already seated on a comfortable couch waiting their turn and smoking their morning cigarette whilst discussing any snippet of news that has come via the outside working parties, been read in the Daily Mirror, or had been said by the Commandant or one of the interpreters. I wait to be shaved, and then progress through the scenery door to the reading room proper.

Already there are a number of prisoners gathered round the fire with their books. I sit at the table and try to learn some new English words and do a translation exercise from my Gaspey-Sauer[40], from which the beautiful map of England has already been torn to prevent me using it, should I attempt to escape.

Despite the stove, the room is still cold, and after an hour, I head outside and run up and down the tarmacked road in an effort to get warm. Then I remember that I have asked the Arts & Crafts workshop to make me a small jewel box to give to my fiancée when I return home. I will see if it is finished. It is not finished yet, but I can see her initials skilfully inlaid into the dark wood. Perhaps it is as well that it still needs work on it as I have not yet received the money order I requested from home three months ago to enable me to pay for it.

The men are working on all sorts of wonderful things - cigarette cases, photo frames, toys of every description including gaudily painted rocking parrots. If only I had money to spare, but how would I manage to carry everything back home with me?

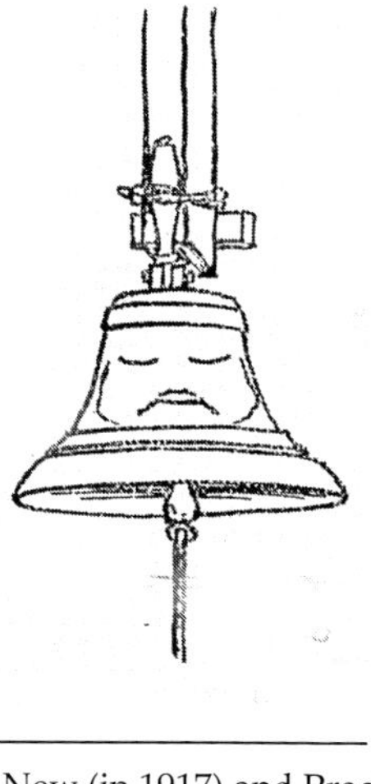

My next port of call is to the canteen shop where I enquire if they have a pair of inner soles which would help to keep my feet dry and warm until my boots are repaired.

[40] A New (in 1917) and Practical Method of Learning a Foreign Language introduced by Otto Gaspey-Sauer.

But no, they have not been available this year! How about a pair of woollen gloves? No joy again. Then I ask, in the hope that I might get some inner warmth, "When is the next delivery of our cigarette ration due?" "Perhaps on Saturday" was the reply from the jolly assistant. Today is only Tuesday and I have only ten cigarettes left! I don't ask for food as there is never anything to be had. I look around to see what they are selling – shaving things, brushes, mirrors, soap, boot polish and shoe laces. I buy a tin of boot polish and leave the shop knowing that due to the lack of supplies, I have saved a lot of money!

Returning to the reading room, I can occupy myself in several ways: learning English or French, shorthand, book-keeping or other important things. My growing hunger is temporarily suppressed by smoking two of my ten cigarettes. Before long a notice appears in the library to say "English papers have arrived". I collect a paper and try my best with my beginner's knowledge to translate the political reports while I wait anxiously for the kitchen bell, as the pangs of hunger are affecting my concentration.

Eventually I hear the bell and return to my hut. Others come from all directions; some have been cleaning pathways and unloading coal, others doing the washing which, as the rain has stopped, is now hanging on lines, hoping it will dry in the remaining hours of day light. A few had been to the Hospital for treatment or a massage, whilst others have been paying their respects at the burial of a dead comrade. And some had just spent the morning lying on their beds reading novels!

Now the large dishes of food appear. This is our main meal of the day, and each of us receives his bowl three quarters full with mashed potatoes, a few peas or beans and a small piece of bacon. The only noise is that of eating implements scraping every last scrap from our bowls. A voice breaks the silence, "Another bowl full would not cause me any stomach troubles." No-one disagrees.

Funeral Service for a German Soldier

Reproduced courtesy of Dr M Cox

One of our number sneaks out to see if he can get a glimpse of the daily list, published at noon, of those who are to receive parcels or money orders today. He returns to say that five of us are lucky, and I am one of them! The extent of my happiness cannot be measured as my long awaited money order has at last arrived. The parcels will be issued at two o'clock so, while some have a mid-day snooze, I spend some time back in the reading room. I make myself comfortable in one of the arm chairs and immerse myself in the treasures of our beautiful literature, offered to us by the camp library, thanks to the generous donation of books from Germany.

The time goes slowly until two o'clock and then I join the long line of parcel receivers who crowd outside the back entrance to the Post Office. Every man has a box, a kit bag, or a towel with him ready to receive his parcel. The original wrapping is not to be issued to us as it may contain some secret message or map. The queue moves slowly forward and eventually it is my turn. A long cardboard box with a sewn canvas cover appears on the distribution table. I can see at a glance that it is from home.

The packaging is cut with a sharp knife and then a Post Orderly makes an exact note of the contents I am about to receive. First there is a loaf, or it was a loaf when it started its journey, but now it is covered in green mould. The oxo cubes are completely squashed and ruined but surprisingly, a packet of biscuits has arrived intact. There are two tins, one of sardines and the orderly removes the label. He then asks what is in the other tin. How should I know? The label appears to be in Danish and no-one is able to translate it! He removes this label also and I am now permitted to go away happy, with my goodies.

As I leave the Post Office the kitchen bell rings, calling us for coffee. I am happy as now, thanks to the donations from home, I can eat my fill. In the hut the stove is crackling away merrily as one of the two weekly distributions of coal has arrived and for a while, everyone feels comfortable and relaxed.

Shortly after three o'clock it's back to the reading room where a packed crowd has gathered, not for studying or reading, but for the distribution of letters. The Postal Officer appears with a big pile and reads out the names again. Much longed for news from home. Thank God my family are all alive and well. My name is called; a card with the Red Cross on it tells me about a parcel that has been sent from Switzerland. There are tins of meat etc. even chocolate. But oh no! On the bottom it says that it could be four months before the parcel arrives, and in four months, I want to be back home!

Distribution of Letters at Brocton

As the distribution of letters is complete, the signal for muster rings out. It is 4 o'clock and everyone lines up again and everything proceeds in the same manner as it did this morning but things go smoothly this time and everyone is present and correct.

The commandant arrives for inspection

Reproduced courtesy of R. Pursehouse

Muster over, I settle down to read by the dim electric light the Camp Newspaper which has just been published. Due to the shortage of paper, the newspaper has become slimmer and slimmer but it still manages to summarise the most important news from the English press.

Now the kitchen bell rings again and bread and sugar are being weighed out on home-made scales and each person is given his allotted portion. Many can't stop themselves from testing the food, although the bread is meant for the next day!

Putting my supplies safely away, I go to the library to look for new books. A queue has formed again and only a few are let in at a time to look through the supply of books. Once they have found something promising they make room for the next man in the queue. One may get himself volumes of Goethe, another an historical work, another some English reading matter, yet another a good modern novel. A lot of them, more modest in their requirement, are satisfied with any Ullstein[41] paperback.

Now it is back to the reading room where, during the afternoon, the billiard table dominates the middle of the room and whenever you are sitting round the table, you have to take great care that you are not unwittingly poked by a billiard cue. The lights are too dim for continuous reading, so I enjoy a game of chess with a comrade and smoke two more of my precious cigarettes.

The sound of the piano comes from the theatre next door where a small choir is rehearsing for the Christmas celebrations. The Camp theatre is used daily, but not always as a means of entertainment. Larger than the normal huts, it has a stage at one end with seating set out for half its length on stepped platforms. At the rear of the seating are scenery "flats" separating the main part of the building from the Barbers Shop, and then through yet more scenery to come to the very popular reading room. By six o'clock the reading room is again crowded, this time for the distribution of money orders. The sum I had expected to receive from home is very much diminished due to the bad rate of exchange. I sign the money order and will receive the cash the day after tomorrow.

[41] German publisher of novels.

A few minutes later the kitchen bell rings again and there is a thin rice soup which completes our rations for the day. In the meantime some of the outside workers have returned laden with large bundles of wood they have collected to add to our stocks of heating material.

At a quarter to seven I'm back in the reading room, which now has a completely changed look. Tables are pushed to the side, chairs and benches are placed in rows and a school blackboard is set up in front of the stove. Our English lesson can begin. It really is too annoying when you are always getting hold of newspapers you cannot read. Therefore a large crowd has assembled to be initiated and informed about the secrets of a foreign language. This is followed by a lesson on the historical development of England, and then a French lesson, but I am too cold to participate in this as well, for the stove must have long since gone out.

I need a brisk walk along the main street to get me warm again. The moon is shining now and again through the clouds and with a magical gleam lights the bare branches of the mighty old oak trees, the most beautiful feature of our camp. My path takes me past the theatre where they are keenly rehearsing and after a gap of many months we are once again to be honoured with a performance.

By the large entrance gates I go to the left for a while, parallel to the barbed wire, and then turn to the large square in the middle of the camp. I pass the bath houses – which unfortunately we are only able to use once every four or five weeks – on past the kitchen, where the lights are being switched off and round I go for another circuit.

I walk round like this for a good hour and then it starts to rain, drumming down on the tin roofs and I am driven back into the hut. Many have already wrapped themselves in blankets, a few are sitting at the table playing cards, and a few are crouched by the stove around which a collection of wet coats and shoes are artistically arranged.

Brocton PoW Camp

At a quarter to ten the signal sounds for everyone to return to their huts and on the second signal at ten o'clock the lights go out. We are again surrounded by complete darkness and the monotonous sound of the rain sends us to sleep. Thank God that another day has gone by and that we are 24 hours nearer to our home land. [42]

[42] Written by an unknown Prisoner of War from Brocton and translated from the German. Doc 6821 IWM

Chapter 9

All in a Day's Work 1918-1919

1918 did not start well for Sir Arthur. After dining at Milford Hall on New Year's Eve he returned to Brocton Leys to celebrate Hogmanay with his family. The maids failed to wake him in the morning and he was late arriving at camp. He was greeted with the news that the prisoners in "F" lines had broken into the stores, done some damage, and stolen food. Coal had also gone missing. Within days the stores were broken into again, this time a quantity of jam and butter went missing. A search revealed some of it, but obviously the rest had already been consumed. Each time food was stolen, rations were cut for everyone, to make up for the stolen items. Those found guilty of stealing were fined 1/- and had their parcels withheld for a month.

January saw 618 prisoners leave in the middle of the night. The Non Commissioned Officers were going to Holland and the wounded to Germany. The NCO's said quite openly that it would be quite easy to slip over the border into Germany once they reached Holland. Many had no money at all, so they were each given 5/- to enable them to get a glass of beer when they arrived. They were also supplied with a meal for the journey. The money was provided by Dr Markel's organisation. Two weeks later another 300 men were sent off to Holland, but each time a group of prisoners left they were replaced by others.

Another large group of prisoners arrived from France. They had large quantities of tobacco, much of it South

African, which they had purchased in an American Canteen in Le Havre. It would appear that even though the war was still raging, the Americans were short of nothing!

The month of February, even in the mildest of years, is usually cold and wet so Sir Arthur was somewhat surprised when, during a routine inspection of the lines, he discovered that all the windows in "E" lines had been broken. He ordered that the glass should be replaced by Friday. If not, money would be taken from anyone who had cash in their account to pay for the repairs! Only a few days later he discovered that the windows in "F" lines had been broken. Again the prisoners were told that, if they failed to repair them, money would be withdrawn from their bank.

Still struggling to get sufficient petrol, Sir Arthur was rather dismayed, when visiting working parties in Rugeley, to meet at least fifteen motor cycles complete with sidecars full of women and children simply joy riding around the Chase! However, his experience in the village of Swynnerton rather pleased him. The little girls curtsied and the boys touched their caps - such good manners after the usual sullen faces and rude stares.

During his travels around the area, Sir Arthur had made the acquaintance of Mr Bostock of Lotus shoes. He wrote to ask the business man if, as they made boots for the army, he could come and view the factory. Mr Bostock replied "I shall be most happy to arrange for you to look over the Lotus Factory at any time that is convenient to yourself. I ought to explain that our Stafford Factory is devoted exclusively to the manufacture of boots & shoes for ladies. Mens boots are made at one of our 2 factories in

Northampton. I am glad you found our ski boots satisfactory when in Switzerland. We were fortunate enough to discover a method of bottoming that makes our boots nearly as water tight as any leather can be. The boots we supply to officers for marching and for field wear are made on the same principal and have given almost universal satisfaction on active service, although worn under most trying conditions."

It had been estimated that over 5,000 farm hands had departed from Staffordshire alone and try as he might, Sir Arthur was unable to meet the demand for agricultural labourers. It was not because he didn't have the workers, he just didn't have sufficient guards!

Since arriving at the Camp, the Commandant had been working hard to establish some sort of order and discipline in the ranks of the R.D.C. They had just all been through a course of musketry, so he was rather distressed to find that at the end of June most of the men were to be sent to Margate, with no reference to him. He would have to start training all over again with a new batch of soldiers. The men of the Royal Engineers also left a lot to be desired. They seem to have very little control over the prisoners they were working with and on one occasion, Sir Arthur found the R.E. Supervisor lying under a tree in the grounds of Brocton Hall asleep, with a handkerchief over his face and a German stretched out beside him!

There was a request in August for accommodation for 1000 wounded men but there was insufficient room for so many. Those who did arrive were smelly and dirty, but appeared to be delighted to be captured. The hospital was now bursting at the seams.

Large parties of prisoners were usually sent away during the night, and in August Sir Arthur decided to travel with a party of 125 men to Boston and see them embark on board ship. After being searched the party left the camp at 2.30 a.m, and then marched down to the station at Milford. The count now showed there were 126 men! The interloper was soon found and returned to camp. He had been questioning those who were leaving to discover all the details of their departure. He needed to be sure he was out of his bed at the right time but the continual questioning of his comrades had given him away! When they reached Boston the following day each prisoner was given a cup of hot coffee by a group of English girls. The men looked utterly miserable, and were reluctant to leave, not knowing what they would find when they reached their destination.

Walton School[43] was to be the venue of a lecture by Sir Arthur at the end of October, and he spent time distributing posters in the hope of attracting a large audience. A week later the lecture was cancelled. The school had been closed on the orders of the Medical Officer as so many pupils were suffering from influenza. The disease was causing quite a panic, and several people in the area had developed pneumonia. Others had died. With so many prisoners suffering from flu, and the number of wounded prisoners increasing daily, "B" lines had to be given up to the hospital.

---

[43] This school at the bottom of School Lane, Walton on the Hill, is now a Children's Nursery.

Sir Arthur at Monymusk

Reproduced by courtesy of Sir Archibald & Lady Fiona Grant

Within a fortnight of the armistice, a general election was called to take place on 14th December. Sir Arthur was anxious to vote and made three journeys into Stafford in just one day, to try and ascertain from Mr Joy, his friend and Clerk to the County Council, whether he would be allowed to vote in Stafford. Perhaps the Government had not thought things through, but if Sir Arthur wished to vote he would have to go to Scotland. Soldiers serving overseas were able to cast their votes, but many men and women working in this country, and far from home, could not afford the time or the money to travel back to base to vote.

Although this was the first time some women and all men over 21 were eligible to vote, the turn-out was only 57%. Sir Arthur travelled north to cast his vote and took the opportunity to enjoy some fishing and shooting on his estate.

The PoWs were busy working all over the local area and Sir Arthur appeared to have everything under control. However it was a little different in the New Zealand lines. Their Colonel had been trying to instil a little discipline into his men but his efforts were not appreciated. The Kiwi's, or at least some of them, were not at all keen to do any "soldiering" now that the armistice had been signed, and there was what amounted to a riot, resulting in £2,000 worth of damage. Three soldiers even tried to hang their Colonel! British troops, anxious to be demobbed and return to civilian life, also demonstrated in London.

In January 1919, with the War over, prisoners were still complaining to the Swiss Legation. This time it was because they had no note paper on which to write home. Prisoners were allowed to write, free of charge, two letters a week, and they could receive unlimited letters and parcels from home. However, all outgoing letters had to be written on a special paper designed to prevent the use of secret inks! Envelopes had a heading "Prisoner of War" and in the top right "No Stamp Required".

All letters, both incoming and outgoing, were censored, and once opened were marked with a stamp saying "Passed by Censor". Any which contained complaints of ill treatment were withheld and returned to the Commandant of the Camp from which they came. Useful information was gained from incoming letters which told of conditions in Germany. Despite the prisoner's grievances, the Swiss Legation reported that they were impressed with conditions prevailing at Brocton Camp and Hospital.

The Commandant continued his daily round of inspecting huts and working parties. Fifty PoWs were kept busy filling in the training trenches on the Chase and on the whole, things were clean, with the prisoners working well. It was not the same elsewhere. The miners were on strike, holding the rest of the country to ransom, while there were reports that coal could be landed in the country from overseas cheaper than it could be provided locally. A ton of coal now cost 6/6d making it almost out of the reach of the poor. It also had an adverse effect on industry. An inspection of "F" lines found that the cook had not only been stealing coal, but had been burning bones! He was removed from the cookhouse straight to the cells!

Sir Arthur was told by employers that PoWs working as fitters and motor mechanics surpassed our men both in ability and hard work.

At Easter 1919, the weather was warm and sunny, and the Chase was crowded with people from the nearby towns. The fair was back on Milford Common for the first time since the end of the war. There appeared to be an additional attraction this time. A number of "professional" ladies were hanging about, each anxious to catch the eye of a good looking New Zealand soldier!

Further complaints from the prisoners were investigated by Lt Col. Thornhill who found that "The Camp is extremely well run and the comfort and convenience of the prisoners ensured. The general discipline of the Camp is excellent. The Commandant is a strong, kind hearted man and a strict disciplinarian. He has managed a very difficult camp with consummate success."[44]

[44] IWM Doc 6821

This report contrasts greatly with documents written by certain prisoners on their return home. They complained about the poor quality of their housing, which was exactly the same as that lived in by British and New Zealand soldiers training on the Chase, and about their "draconian commandant".

One prisoner wrote after the war "I don't think England was ever more roundly cursed than at Brocton. It is known among all the prisoners as the worst and most hunger stricken. We lay in barracks where the dampness ran down the walls, with the thermometer down to freezing without coal"

Another dramatic account says "Fifteen of us, all on crutches, came together in a barrack. The Commandant tormented us to the utmost. We men on crutches had to scrub and carry water just like the others. And if we didn't, he would lock us up. The Commandant sometimes shot into the floor next to us. When he felt like doing so he would furnish no coal, or post a notice saying "Meals will be omitted today". Our mail would be held back until the contents of the packages were spoiled."

This report seems very dramatic and it contrasts greatly with reports of prisoners being reluctant to leave and others writing to the Commandant thanking him for his kindness.

After a hundred years it is difficult to say exactly how well the prisoners were treated. A British Lieutenant Colonel tells us that all is well, whilst some Germans who spent time confined in the Camp say otherwise. Perhaps we should reflect upon a report by the Swiss Legation as being unbiased. It states "Brocton Camp is among the best we have visited so far. The arrangements are excellent. The Commandant, Lt. Colonel Sir Arthur Grant unites strict military discipline with kindness and takes a personal interest in the welfare of the prisoners under his charge."

Chapter 10

Food

When War broke out in 1914, there was a mad rush to buy and stock-pile food. By the end of August 1914, some stores had empty shelves but the public soon realised that food would not keep for ever, and before long everything returned to normal.

However, in 1917 the Germans started to attack ships bringing supplies to Britain in an attempt to starve us into submission. By early that year there was a shortage of potatoes, and the Parliamentary Secretary to the Ministry of Food announced in the House of Commons in March that there was a real "possibility that the stock of potatoes would be exhausted before the 1917 supplies were available. Therefore, an increased price was allowed for potatoes delivered after 31st March, with the object of giving an inducement to growers not to throw the whole of their supplies upon the market at once. There was no intention of establishing a system of compulsory rations, in the case of potatoes."

One MP commented that a number of retailers were refusing to supply potatoes at the stipulated price of 1½d. per lb. unless other vegetables were purchased at the same time and seeing that this practice entailed hardship on the poor, wondered whether immediate steps should be taken to render it illegal?[45] "Such cases are to be investigated," came the reply. However, within a month, an order was in place to prohibit the use of potatoes in hotels. Again questions were asked in the House. "Would the new order preventing the serving of potatoes in hotels be extended to those establishments occupied by Germans?"

Despite the shortages, the PoWs continued to receive 4 ounces of potato per day and before long this was increased to 20 ounces per day! The Prisoners at Brocton were always looking for a reason to complain and aware that their potato ration had been increased by Army Council Instructions,

---

[45] Hansard 1st March 1917

they were quick to protest when they did not immediately receive their new ration.

It took five days before the required amount of potatoes could be delivered to the Camp - quite long enough for them to register a complaint and make a fuss!

German Prisoners Peeling Potatoes at Brocton

Reproduced by courtesy of Dr M. Cox

Evie Grant also protested to her husband! She wrote "Why do you feed your Huns on potatoes? My baby can't have any and weeps gallons when he has to have his dinner without. We've had several potato-less days lately. Couldn't you send us down a sack of potatoes?"

The sinking, by Germany, of ships bringing food to Britain was beginning to have an effect and by February 1918, tea, margarine or butter and meat were rationed. Sugar followed in March.

German Prisoners planting potatoes

An article in the "Sunday Chronicle" on 1st July 1918 by "one who knows the facts" details the daily amounts of food allocated to German prisoners – Meat 6ozs, Cheese 4ozs, Bread 13ozs, Potatoes 20ozs, Fresh Vegetables 4ozs, Peas, Beans, Rice, Oatmeal 4½ozs, Margarine 1oz, Jam 1oz, Tea ½oz and sugar 1oz." He goes on to say that "German prisoners get more meat, more cheese, more jam, and more margarine, than the average amount that can be obtained per head by our own people. He gets practically the same amount of sugar and tea, and more potatoes, fresh and dry vegetables, rice, etc. than is consumed by the average person. Compare this with the predicament of our own unfortunate men in Germany.

In December last, although the prisoners received 7oz of margarine weekly, an order was issued from London that all Germans doing hard work should be given an additional margarine ration of 7 oz. per head per week if certified by the camp Medical Officer. Imagine a weekly ration of 14 oz. of margarine each to healthy prisoners at a time when we could, with difficulty, procure about 4 oz. each for our own free people."

Chief Constable George Anson

A story says that Prisoners were for some time receiving the very best Hartley's jam in jars while British men and officers were having to put up with tinned "jam," a mixture of vegetable pulp and fruit "flavouring".

The prisoners from Brocton were allowed to go into Stafford under guard, giving them an ideal opportunity to spend any money they may have had. Their spending habits resulted in the Chief Constable contacting the Press and asking them to publish the following statement. "We are requested by the Chief Constable of Staffordshire to call attention to the fact that Prisoners of War in this country are particularly prohibited from acquiring or attempting to acquire any food of the following description – Meat, of any description whatever, including bacon or ham, poultry etc. sugar or any article of which sugar is an ingredient such as jam, sweets etc. and flour or any article of which flour is an ingredient.

Prisoners of War are not allowed to have a larger amount of the above foods than is obtainable by or laid down as sufficient for the civilian population in this country unless they receive it from abroad.

Anyone who assists a prisoner to break this regulation is liable to the full penalty of imprisonment and fine attached to any breach of the Defence of the Realm regulations. Shopkeepers and others are warned against having any unauthorised dealings of any sort with any Prisoner of War, or with their escorts as any such dealings may lead to trouble.

Prisoners of War in this country are well fed, well clothed, and kindly treated. Our fellow countrymen who are prisoners in Germany are starved and treated with brutal cruelty and it is unfair to them to show any special favour to the German prisoners in this country."[46]

Perhaps it was this article that prompted Mr H. Pyrah of Stafford to write to Sir Arthur, and the Press in the following terms:- "To save further annoyance to ourselves and also to the English men who are compelled to escort them, we shall be obliged if you will place our shop out of bounds to all German prisoners, otherwise the next entrant will likely meet with something more than forcible words."

[46] "The Mercury, 24th May 1918

As the Pyrah's ran a Ladies Corsetry Shop in Greengate Street, one wonders just what the German prisoners were doing there in the first place!

Prisoners at Brocton often complained about their food despite them having no reason to protest. To them it was just a means of making things difficult for the guards and the Commandant. Fresh milk was available from local farms, and Margaret Smallwood recalls how a German, accompanied by a British guard, would come each morning to their small holding in Brocton to collect milk for the Senior German Officers.[47]

The prisoners also collected acorns from the oaks in Brocton Coppice which they roasted and said they were very good! One prisoner, feeling rather hungry, wrote to the Commandant saying that if he was offered an Iron Cross or a piece of Bread of the same size he would choose the bread![48]

At Brocton Camp nothing was wasted. Crumbs and stale bread, if there ever was any, were baked in huge ovens and sold to Birmingham manufacturers of calves' food; bones, fat, marrow, crackling, meat-residue, swill, and even paper, were disposed of for good money in the best markets.

Christmas 1917 saw the prisoners receive additional rations in the form of 32 cwt of apples, 1266 packets of soup, 4 lbs of Nutmeg and 2538 lbs of horseflesh. To complete the festivities, each hut had a Christmas tree and the men were allowed to decorate the huts with boughs of holly, ivy and other greenery that they could collect close to Camp.

---

[47] Down Memory Lane compiled by J. Foley.

[48] A 1914 Iron Cross is approx. 42mm square

It was reported just before Christmas 1917 that there was a 2 year supply of coffee in England and only 2 month's supply of tea but the food controller did not want to recommend people drink coffee as it required more milk!

Meanwhile, the authorities were advising the local population to "Eat slowly: you will need less food" and "Keep warm: you will need less food". Keeping warm was difficult as most of the coal being mined was used to keep the factories running for the war effort. As Christmas drew near, the Ministry of Food planned a patriotic Christmas dinner for the British population consisting of French rice soup, filleted haddock, roast fowl and vegetables, followed by plum pudding at an estimated cost of 10/2d for four people. This was wishful thinking as a chicken would cost at least 10/- in town. Perhaps the country folk would have more luck!

A German Christmas Card

Deutsche Zeitung

Nr. 359. Broctonlager, den 25. Dezember 1918. 2. Jahrg.

Weihnachten 1918

Brich an, du schönes Morgenlicht!
Das ist der alte Morgen nicht,
der täglich wiederkehret.
Es ist ein Leuchten aus der Fern',
es ist ein Schimmer, ist ein Stern,
von dem ich längst gehöret.

Der Himmel ist jetzt nimmer weit,
es naht die selge Gotteszeit
der Freiheit und der Liebe.
Wohlauf, du frohe Christenheit!
daß jeder sich nach langem Streit
in Friedenswerken übe.

Max von Schenkendorf

Christmas Newspaper 1918

Chapter 11

Entertainment

With so many men confined within the Camp it was important to keep them amused or, at least, allow them to keep themselves amused!

Brocton Camp had a fine theatre with a stage at one end, in front of which was tiered seating. The rear of the theatre was used during the day and when not required in the evening, as the Barber's Shop and the Reading Room.

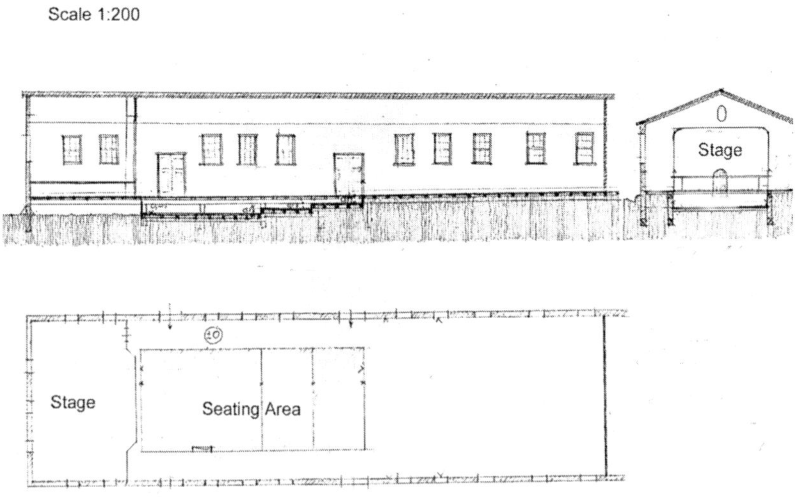

Brocton PoW Camp Theatre

The theatre was used regularly. Records show that, during the first year of its existence, the drama group performed on 81 evenings and in its second year, on 61 evenings. Often performances had to be repeated on consecutive evenings to meet the demand for seats!

Perhaps one of the very first performances in the theatre was a dancing display entitled "The Enchanted Glen" by the students of dance teacher, Miss Martha Stichling of Stafford.

Although Martha and her brother Charles were born in London, both their parents were German, so Martha was more than keen to offer help with entertaining the German prisoners when the Camp opened in 1917. Mrs Stichling and her children remained in Stafford during the war, but there is no trace of her husband at this time. It is possible that he was interred for the duration, maybe at Knockaloe Camp on the Isle of Man. At the outbreak of war, with the German-owned Siemens Brothers Dynamo Works Ltd. being a major employer in the town, there were many German families in the area. The works had opened in 1903 bringing over 700 employees from their factory in Woolwich to the town.

The photographs on the previous page show seven year old Eva Davies and her four year old sister, Kathleen, dressed ready to perform in "The Enchanted Garden"

Performers at Brocton Camp

On the Kaiser's birthday, 27th January, there was a performance in the theatre comprising German patriotic songs and speeches. The Commandant attended and reported that there was nothing at all festive about it! However, he did enjoy other concerts produced by the prisoners.

Each dramatic performance seems to have also included musical interludes played by one of the two ensembles from the camp. There was a string orchestra and a brass band. Often, when there was a formal dinner for British officers, a group of musicians would provide back-ground music for the meal. They were rewarded with some beans and ginger beer!

Once again Dr Markel had to be thanked for supplementing camp funds and helping to provide some of the instruments and costumes for each performance. Sir Arthur had been responsible for locating a piano for the theatre.

Easter 1918 saw a performance of "St John's Eve Fire" by dramatist and novelist Herman Sudermann take place in the theatre. Billed as a drama in four acts, it appears to have been reminiscent of a Brian Rix farce! It must have caused great amusement amongst the prisoners. The plot revolved around two beautiful women and a handsome young man who was planning to marry one, despite really loving the other! In its English translation there are two extracts which would have caused great laughter from the audience. The first says "I find the whole world beautiful; but the surroundings here are exceptionally so. Yes, this place to me seems doubly attractive, for here every one seems smiling and happy" The second quote says "I tell you, Pastor, it was months before we could rid the blankets of vermin."

The performance of St John's Eve Fire was followed by music by Gounod, Tchaikovsky, and Mendelssohn.

The cast of "St John's Eve Fire"

Reproduced by courtesy of Dr M. Cox

On Saturday 18th January, 1919, the thespians performed "Moral" by Bavarian playwright Ludwig Thoma (a nom de plume: as his real name was Peter Schlemihl.) This was a comedy with, once again, the challenge for some of the actors to portray beautiful young ladies!

The following evening the theatre saw the Camp's "First Chamber Music Evening", with performances of music by Mendelssohn, Schubert, and Richard Strauss among others. This concert was much more ambitious than the musical interludes which accompanied the theatrical performances and was no doubt the result of many hours of practice.

A Musical Interlude following St John's Eve Fire"

Reproduced by courtesy of Dr M. Cox

Other prisoners with a musical bent would join the choir and as the orchestra was known to have played the overture to the "Mikado", perhaps there were plans for a performance of this Gilbert & Sullivan operetta.

Photographic postcards of various performances were sent by Alfred Grosshennig to his family in Cologne or to his lady friend Hilde Oertel. He was a prisoner of war from 1915 until 1919, coming to Brocton in October 1917. He would remain in Staffordshire until he was repatriated in 1919.

Alfred can be seen in the picture on the following page ready, we believe, to prompt a performance, while his comrades seem anxious to have a taste of the wurst sausage he is holding!

Reproduced by courtesy of Dr M. Cox

Opposite the prisoners are pictured in a scene from "Old Heidelberg" by Wilhelm Meyer-Forster, their Christmas performance in 1917. The play was written in 1901 and tells of a prince studying at Heidelberg University who falls in love with an inn-keeper's daughter. When his father dies, the prince has to return home as King and marry a royal princess. The play was later turned into a light opera, "The Student Prince" by Sigmond Romberg.

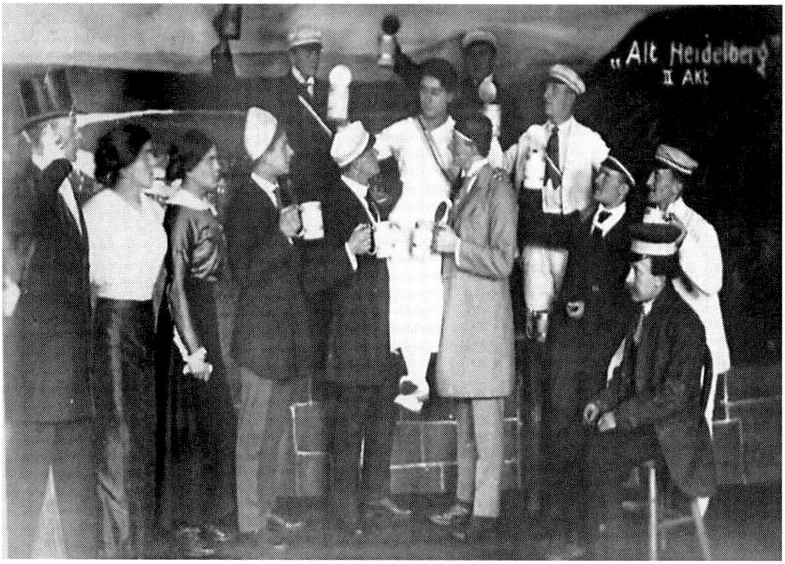

A Scene from "Old Heidelberg"

Reproduced courtesy of Dr M Cox

Another play, "The White Horse Inn" written and first staged in 1897, was performed by the prisoners in 1919. Again it is a comedy with a love theme, and gave the chance for some lucky prisoner to play the part of a beautiful young woman! This play was later translated into English and became a very popular operetta in the 1930's. The actors were all presented with a diploma signed by Sir Arthur to commemorate their performance.

The ingenuity of the prisoners was evident at a Fancy Dress Ball held in March 1919. The costumes were very good, and the event was described as "quite amusing" with everyone enjoying themselves despite the lack of real female partners!

The Cast of the "White Horse Inn"

Reproduced courtesy of Dr M Cox

The reading-room at the rear of the theatre contained two billiard tables, had been decorated and hung with pictures painted by talented prisoners. Small tables and easy chairs allowed prisoners to play chess and other board games, provided for the most part by Dr Markel. The billiard tables were never empty but those playing other games on the small tables had to be careful that they were not hit by a billiard cue.

For the more energetic, there were regular games of football between the various huts and by September 1917 they had a gymnasium to help them keep fit. Prisoners originally were allowed to walk on the Chase for their enjoyment - but always under guard. This form of exercise was not particularly popular and as it involved deploying several guards, was eventually discontinued!

If a prisoner wanted to walk, he had to walk around the internal perimeter of the Camp - about one and a quarter miles.

A Prisoners Football team

Reproduced courtesy of Graham Mark

Religion also played an important part in Camp life. A Lutheran Minister and teacher of history, Dr Gerhard Günzel had been captured at Ypres in 1914. After a spell in Jersey he was moved to Brocton where he remained until his release in September 1919.

A photograph of Gerhard was sent from Brocton in May 1918 and shows him surrounded by books and in good health.

Dr Gerhard Gunzel

It was obviously not taken in his living quarters, but perhaps in a hut designated as a Church or Chapel for the prisoners, where he could prepare his sermons and give advice and support to fellow country-men. Gerhard sent no message home on this postcard apart from the information that he was in "A" lines, Hut 12. Perhaps this was a plea for letters from home.

The camp newspapers especially at Christmas, Easter and other religious festivals, discussed the trials and tribulations of war and captivity with fervent hopes that it would soon all come to an end.

Along with expressions of patriotism the articles link Easter and the coming of Spring to the overwhelming desire to return to their families and the resumption of a life of peace far away from the death and destruction of war. The writings are clearly educated and often poetic, perhaps the product of Gerhard Gunzel's pen.

Chapter 12

Escapes, Shootings and Death

Sentries watch over working prisoners

Did the barbed wire, tall fences and the sentries prevent any escapes? They did not! On 5th February, 1918 four prisoners, Emil Schnieder, Herman Gerwin, Joseph Koch and Robert Liebeg escaped dressed in civilian clothing.[49] One wonders how they managed to acquire sufficient clothing to kit them all out in such a manner that they did not look suspicious.

[49] Birmingham Daily Post 8th February, 1918

It is recorded that prisoners helped with gardening for elderly local people such as old Mrs Trundley of Walton Village. Jemima Trundley was a widow whose only son was killed in September 1917. Knowing how cold it could be on the Chase, perhaps she, or someone like her, thought they were doing the Germans a favour by giving them warm clothing that would no longer be needed by their son or husband. Or maybe their outfits were just stolen from a washing line!

The prisoners were not missed until the Canteen Manager, Mr Green, arrived at Camp on the morning of the 6th February. He had noticed a bundle of prisoner's clothes outside the wire, a fact he reported immediately to the Commandant. It was discovered that the wire had been cut at a point where Sir Arthur had always said was the most likely point someone would try to get out. After cutting the wire, they just crawled through, changed into civilian clothes and they were free! The following day there was a full roll call of all prisoners to establish who had escaped. Their names and descriptions were then reported to various Government departments.

Emil Schnieder was vital to the escape plan, as he spoke fluent English and was a sailor. The authorities must have considered him to be the ring leader, as they issued a detailed description of him to the Press. Aged 29, with black hair and brown eyes, he was just 5ft 6 inches tall with a mole on his right cheek.

Everything must have been well planned, for two days later the four had made their way to Halesworth, Suffolk, not far from Ipswich where they were eventually captured and returned to Brocton. They had travelled over 160 miles from Camp and when caught had been less than eight miles from the coast. They were obviously hoping, with Emil's knowledge, to be able steal a vessel or stow away on a ship going to Belgium, Holland or even Germany.

On their return to Brocton the Commandant had the four "tourists" up before him. They were questioned and it would appear that they had been planning their escape for some time. They cut the wire under cover of darkness at about 7.30 p.m. and then walked to Stafford station. Catching a bus or train from Milford would be too dangerous, as the locals were very much aware of the Germans on the Chase and villagers would immediately spot four strangers. A man at Stafford station had been suspicious of the four and he expressed his concern to the ticket inspector who told him to "mind his own business." By this time the escapees had boarded a train and were on their way south. Walking through the village of Halesworth, they were spoken to by a curious civilian, who wondered who they were and what they were doing. Three of the men said they were engineers, the fourth said that he was an "Engine". The game was up and they were arrested and returned to Brocton!

As a punishment the Commandant stripped the men and put them into the dirtiest old clothes he could find, put a large basket on each of their heads as punishment and then sent them out to work. He reported that the four looked very miserable, but they had caused him a great deal of worry. However, he was cheered that same morning by the receipt of a letter from the War Office quoting a report from a speech in the Reichstag. It said that Brocton was in a very charming location and that the Commandant took a lively interest in the Prisoners of War, more so than at any other Camp.

Later the Commandant heard rumours that when they left camp the four escapees had over £60 in notes in their possession. No matter how hard he tried, he could not discover if this were true and if it was, where had the money come from and where was it hidden? Green, the Canteen Manager, was rewarded for alerting the Camp of the escape and given £1.

A month later, 20 year old, Paul Drescher decided to abscond from his working party. With no preparation, this was not a good idea, and he only made it as far as Rugeley, less than five miles from Brocton, before he was captured. He was brought back to camp the following day. P.C. Batkin, the local policeman at Milford, was always on the lookout for unfamiliar faces. Since the start of the war he had spent many hours helping to escort Prisoners from Milford and Brocton Station to the Camp, and he was particularly keen that they stayed there! He had enough to do sorting out problems with the troops who drank too much in the Barley Mow without having to go looking for escaped prisoners!

Or that is the story as reported in the Press, but it was not quite like that. Drescher disappeared whilst working in Rugeley and a search was made for him without success. However, two days later he was found sitting in a hut smoking his pipe, just where he had been working when he "disappeared". When questioned he claimed that he had no intention of escaping, he just wanted to cause the British trouble! The Commandant described him as a blaggard!

Despite his claim, Paul Drescher did want to get away. In February 1919 he escaped from Retford Camp, Nottinghamshire, one of Brocton's satellite agricultural camps, along with his friend Adam Acker. Neither man could speak English. Some days later Drescher was discovered hiding on board a French steamer at Grimsby. He was taken back to Retford but, on 7th March, he escaped for a second time. On this occasion he managed to get as far as Blyth, Northumberland, after yet again boarding a boat in Grimsby. He was discovered, and the Blyth authorities handed him over to a military escort. Drescher was soon on his way back to Retford by train. When the train stopped at Doncaster station, he took his chance, leapt out of the window on to the railway line, and ran away. He escaped without his boots, wearing a green felt Trilby hat, grey tunic and trousers over his prisoner of war uniform! He did not stand a chance and was eventually found in a railway wagon and returned to Retford Camp. It is doubtful if he was allowed out on working parties ever again!

By July 1919 many Germans had been repatriated, but there were two prisoners at Brocton who could not wait for the formalities to be completed. Dressed in their working clothes Gustav Hohendoff (39) and Johann Reuter (28) escaped from Brocton. In an effort to see them recaptured the War Office released their descriptions. Hohendoff was 5 feet 9 inches tall, of fresh complexion, with brown hair and eyes. His companion was 5 feet 6 inches tall with fair hair and blue eyes and a wound mark on his right leg. Were they ever recaptured? We do not know.

This however, was not the last of the escapes from the camp. On 20th August, 1919, Otto Saalfeld, aged 32, escaped in full dress uniform![50] Another escapee was Paul Bookel. We do not know how long he had been at large, but on 9th September, 1919 it was reported in the Western Times that Bookel, from Brocton Camp, had been recaptured! The fear of being shot by a guard as they escaped did not seem to deter some prisoners although they most probably escaped by just quietly slipping away when no-one was looking, when out with a working party.

There were occasions when it was feared that a prisoner was about to escape. In October 1918 a sentry shot at a prisoner who was "hanging about the wire" but no harm was done and the prisoner quickly returned to his work. However, on the same day at about 10.45 p.m. there was the sound of gun fire. Immediately the Commandant was out of his bed, thinking that the same prisoner was attempting a getaway. The sentry had shot a deer that had come to eat acorns close to wire! At twelve paces he could not miss and the poor animal was dead.

There then ensued a battle between the Commandant and the R.D.C. over the ownership of the carcass. The meat was very good and enjoyed by the Commandant and the doctors!

On 24th January, 1918 Sir Arthur wrote in his pocket diary "One Prisoner of War shot through bottom". The

[50] Sheffield Evening Telegraph

shooting was investigated and the reporting officer was a little more delicate in his description of events. "I beg to report that at 3.40 p.m., this day, a Prisoner of War, Georg Wilhelm, was fired upon by No 34893 Private D. Rands of this Company who was on sentry duty patrolling the space known as "the run" which divides "E" & "F" Prisoners of War Compounds, and a flesh wound was inflicted.

I have had the sentry before me, and he states that the wounded prisoner was speaking across "the run" to prisoners in the other compound when the sentry ordered him to go away from the wire fence, close to which he was standing. The prisoner abused him and would not move, and the sentry repeatedly warned the prisoner that, unless he obeyed the order, he would be fired upon. In response to these warning the prisoner continued to abuse him, and "make faces" at the sentry who eventually fired and inflicted a flesh would. Other PoWs in one compound then threw missiles (bricks etc.) at the sentry. The other sentry on duty in "The Run" at the time confirms the above statement."

Things were much more serious on 27th February, 1919. Twenty year old Karl Kabolleck, a Private in the 65th Bavarian Infantry Regiment who had been at Brocton just three months, was shot and killed by Arthur Gent of the Northumberland Fusiliers close to the Cook House of "F" lines. Gent had been a prisoner of war in Germany for several months and had seen the treatment given out to British would be escapees. Perhaps he did not think twice before he fired. The following day a Court of Inquiry into the shooting was held at the Camp. However, the whole procedure had to be repeated as at the original inquiry the

Court had omitted to hear the Medical Officer's evidence and that meant that in the eyes of the army, Karl Kabolleck was not "officially dead".

An inquest was held in Stafford on 3rd March by the Coroner, Mr S.W. Morgan, and the findings were that Kabolleck died from shock due to a rifle shot wound in the abdomen caused by Private Gent firing at him whilst on sentry duty. The Verdict was returned as, Justifiable homicide.[51]

At about 3.45 p.m. Kabolleck, accompanied by a Hungarian PoW named Mihaly, was supposedly picking

potatoes close to the boundary wire. The sentry was of the opinion that he was trying to get under the wire. The sentry called out "Weg, Weg" (Away, Away)

several times and the prisoner was returning to the correct side of the wire when the sentry fired. He fell over the wire and shrieked out. Private Gent said he had seen that particular prisoner earlier in the afternoon put his head round the corner of the cookhouse and when he

[51] Coroners Records Stafford Record Office.

(Kabolleck) realised he had been seen, he went away. Later he was seen bending over the drain inside the wire. Private Gent was of the opinion that the prisoner was about to attempt an escape and it was his duty to obey orders and prevent any breakouts. He was about 9 yards away from the prisoner when he fired.

Captain Warner of the Royal Army Medical Corps was summoned, and found the prisoner lying on his back on the ground dead with a severe wound to the abdomen. Death would have been almost immediate.[52]

The jury found that no blame could be attributed to the sentry, and that his actions were justifiable. The explanation that Kabolleck was picking potatoes seems rather strange in February. If the prisoners had planted potatoes to supplement their diet, they should have long since been harvested and it was far too early to be planting next season's crop! Perhaps he was trying to escape and the potatoes had been deliberately dropped to give a reason to crouch down, with the intention that when he was sure that the sentry was looking the other way he could get under the wire.

However, at the request of German Camp Leader Schule, the case was investigated by the Swiss Legation. A letter to the Commandant states "I am convinced, particularly by the fact that Kabolleck's body was found in the compound, that at the moment he was shot he was not defying the sentry's challenge "to get out," but, on the contrary, was on the point of obeying the challenge, if he had not practically already succeeded in doing so. I cannot help

52 Report in the Staffordshire Advertiser, March 1919.

wondering if it might have been possible for the sentry to aim at him in such a manner that his life at least would have been spared."

Karl was buried in the Military Cemetery at Broadhurst Green. An acre of land had been given by the Earl of Lichfield in January 1917 for such a cemetery[53]. By March the Military Authorities reported that they had accepted a quote for fencing the area and the paths and drains would be constructed as soon as possible using military labour. Rugeley Burial Board was anxious for the work to be completed as so many military funerals were putting pressure on the community's cemetery. Forty-three such burials had taken place since the start of the war, and this was before the arrival of the Prisoners of War in April 1917. Over 200 prisoners died between 1917 and 1919.[54] Two, Claus Carstens and Friedrich Grimm, committed suicide by hanging. Alfred Vogel, aged just 26, collapsed while out with a working party and died of a heart attack. There was mystery surrounding the death of Karl Langer. He suffered a fracture to the base of his skull, but there was insufficient evidence to indicate how it happened. Was it an accident, or was it murder by one of his compatriots with no one prepared to spill the beans? Some died from their injuries, but the majority of the rest died during the 1918 influenza epidemic and are buried in the Military Cemetery on Cannock Chase.

[53] Karl and his fellow Prisoners of War are buried in the Military Cemetery and not in the German Cemetery close by. The dedication of the German Cemetery did not take place until June 1967.

[54] A list of those who died can be found in the appendix.

Keeping fresh air in the huts had led to many battles between the Commandant and the prisoners but by October 1918 Sir Arthur knew he was right to insist that the windows were kept open. At the end of the month there were 200 cases of influenza in "E" & "F" lines where, whenever they could get away with it, the windows were closed. "A" lines, the residents of which always seemed to obey all the rules had none. Just three days later there were 280 cases in "E" & "F" lines but still none in "A" lines. Unfortunately, Sir Arthur suffered a very mild attack of flu which he claimed he had picked up from inspecting the lines. The doctor treated him with castor oil! Within three days Sir Arthur was up and about again and he received permission to cut off the tobacco ration to lines "E" & "F" as punishment for disobeying orders and failing to keep the windows open.

Perhaps Sir Arthur should not have been in such a hurry to return to work as, a few days later, he was again under the weather and feeling weak. When peace was declared on 11th November, he had to stay in bed and could not join in any of the celebrations. The prisoners were all very down hearted saying that the Kaiser must go and a republic created in Germany.

Sir Arthur took a few days leave, hoping the sea air in Bournemouth would help him recover from his illness. On his way back to Brocton he had an appointment at the War Office and then he and Evie walked down the Mall to look at the German guns of all sorts and sizes that were displayed there. Most had sand or half bricks down the breeches, a reflection of what the British Public thought of the Germans!

He returned to Brocton in time to attend the burial on 29th November of eleven prisoners who all died from the effects of influenza. Although others had died during the previous two months, there had never been so many to be interred on one day.

The Military Cemetery, Cannock Chase 2015

The last four months of 1918 saw 132 Prisoners die mainly from Spanish 'flu, and it was not until April of the following year that the authorities were able to record a death free-month. The epidemic was over and life in camp returned to normal.

Chapter 13

Going Home?

In June 1917 a delegation from Britain met with German Officers at The Hague to discuss the treatment and possible exchange of prisoners to a neutral country. It was reported to the House of Commons that the delegation, comprising Lord Newton, General Sir Henry Belfield, and Sir Robert Younger, had powers to discuss the following topics

- The resumption of the repatriation of combatant and civilian prisoners under existing agreements.
- The extension of the existing agreements for the repatriation of combatant and civilian prisoners.
- The transfer of combatant prisoners of war to other neutral countries in addition to Switzerland
- The internment of civilian prisoners of war in neutral countries
- The more expeditious and satisfactory delivery of parcels to prisoners
- The punishment of prisoners
- Reprisals on prisoners
- The delay in reporting and failure to report the capture of prisoners
- The removal of British merchant officers from combatant officers' camps.

Eventually, agreement was reached between the two Governments and arrangements had to be made between Britain,

Holland and Germany, and with the shipping companies concerned, with regard to the steamships which were to convey British prisoners over to Boston, Lincolnshire, and to take German prisoners back. The Prime Minister[55] reported that "I am happy to say that only a day or two ago a telegram arrived stating that these arrangements were almost complete; and so far as His Majesty's Government is concerned, I can state most emphatically that there is no reason whatever why these boats should not start from Holland on any day or at any hour. There will be three steamers employed upon this work and, in accordance with a suggestion made by the German Government, the first trip will be of an experimental character; and as the Germans requested that lying-down cases - cases of invalids should not be dealt with upon this experimental voyage, the prisoners on this first trip will in all probability consist of able-bodied civilians who are exchanged in virtue of old agreements. After the first voyage has taken place, it is to be hoped that it will be followed as soon as possible by other voyages, when incapacitated combatant prisoners will be exchanged."

On 9th January, 1918, 396 prisoners left Brocton for Holland and Germany. Six days later a further 618 left Camp for the Continent.

One of the lucky ones who left Brocton was keen to write to those still in Camp to tell of his experiences of freedom. "When the first party had left, the feeling in camp was very pessimistic as only 175 men left by it. We all worked out which party we would go with and when our turn would come. We could hardly believe that only 175 – 200 men

[55] David Lloyd George

could go each time, but understood why when we got on the ship.

We left Brocton at 6 a.m. after all our luggage had been examined. We arrived the same day in Boston, where we were given our bags and taken at once on board where we were each allotted a berth. Now we were able to move about freely for the first time. We left the harbour on the following day, travelled all that day, and in the evening anchored at the Dutch Lightship. We only continued our journey on the 3rd day and arrived in Koblenz on 27th. We had poor weather on the way, only passed four trading vessels and one Dutch submarine, the latter only 30 yards distance. The journey was made in a most careful manner and every time the ship stopped, beams of wood, lashed together were placed round the ship. These were for protection against mines.

On our arrival we were received with flowers and taken to our quarters by train. We are free always except on Friday for one and a half hours when we have to join our unit for dinner. We are doing ourselves well here and celebrated the Kaiser's birthday fishing. There was a great feast with free beer. We all thought of you and sent you a postcard which we hope you received. I must now close; it is 10 p.m. and time for lights out which here is strictly enforced. Trusting these lines will find you well."

There were constant comings and goings at Brocton. Some Prisoners would be going to Holland or Switzerland as internees for the remainder of the War. Others would just be moving on to another camp where they would be employed in some form of useful work. In February 1918 Edwin Wolff arrived at Brocton Camp.

He would stay only until May when he was sent to Holland as an internee. Once in Holland, he wrote to friends in England complaining of the treatment he had received at Brocton. On arrival he stated that "all his pockets, bags, boxes, valises, and packets were extensively searched and many a thing was flung on the pile of prisoner's property."[56] He claimed his possessions were rifled and looted by British guards, and he was interrogated under threat of torture as well as being ill-treated.

Three Young Germans waiting to go Home

On 18th November 1918, Sir Arthur searched the luggage of six hundred prisoners before they departed for Ripon the following morning. He commented that he found it very necessary to search thoroughly PoWs on their arrival at, and more especially, on their departure from Brocton for repatriation.Many hundred-weights of soap, thousands of socks, shirts and other articles of clothing have thus been retained in this country where they have been badly needed during the war.

[56] IWM Document 4855

However, some were determined not to have their luggage searched. One prisoner wrote "Naturally, we managed to dodge the search by joining and walking along with those men who were carrying their already examined luggage to the guard room. In this manner I managed to get everything through, even the smallest things. I left nothing in England, not even letters and photos, you know what I mean."[57]

Although their life in Brocton had been far better than that of British prisoners in Germany, once away from Staffordshire prisoners were keen to berate the Commandant and his staff.

"Our Commandant was a perfect b****** and locked one up for the merest trifle, even if one was on parade. He constantly told us we were not yet in Holland. We complained to the Swiss Legation, but the Commandant simply tore the letter up before us with the remark, "I am Commandant and not the Swiss". In spite of this, we succeeded in communicating with the Swiss Legation and a representative came down at once. You should have seen the face and fury of the Commandant; anyway he made us suffer for it. Thankful to have got away."

Despite having better food, and more of it, than the locals, prisoners continued to complain about the rations they received.

"We have hungered like the devil. This Commandant (a Scotsman), you know him, gave us only what he thought

[57] Sir Arthur commented that The German has a liking for lewd photographs

proper. Complaints were not entertained, until in a way inexplicable to the English, the Swiss Legation appeared. But we got it in the neck just the same. I can only tell you to remain in Handforth, as nowhere are things more pleasant than where you are, and in any case Handforth is the best place of internment; in Brocton we would have been devouring the horses. On these matters I could fill up an entire sheet, but it is really better not to think about such things.

On the evening of the 26th, we celebrated the Kaiser's birthday in our dining room. The programme was entirely drawn up according to our Peace plans. The necessary eatables, smokes and ladies were there in plenty, so gradually one got back into old ways.

One can go anywhere one likes; buy for money anything one wants. We get our peace time pay according to the peace time rate; also soon we will be given employment. Different comrades have already been to thc Embassy at the Hague. We have all got peace uniforms; for the Infantry a Jaeger uniform, for the Cavalry green and blue Hussars Jackets. There is plenty of movement here, Belgians and Russians are strongly represented. One can find society suitable to one's taste. I have started a very decent friendship with a family, and beer is also drunk pretty well. Therefore, in general, things are going pretty well. I wish you the best of everything."

By February 1919 the Earl of Lichfield was anxious to take control of the Chase once again and he wrote to the War Office asking when the Chase would be returned to him. A reply came back; "A definite promise was made that the

Camp (which the late Lord Lichfield so generously placed at the disposal of the Department) would be dismantled and handed back as soon as possible after the termination of the war. This promise will be carried out and arrangement made to vacate as soon as demobilisation and repatriation of Prisoners of War is sufficiently advanced to allow the Department's evacuation"[58] It took much longer than the Earl had expected and it was not until 1923 before everything had been sold and cleared away from the site.

The prisoners who remained at Brocton were also getting restless. In March 1919 the 2,300 men remaining in "E" and "F" lines wrote a heart-rending appeal requesting their release from their "humiliating position" as a matter of urgency as there was now no military reason for their detention. However, the Germans had still not signed up to the peace terms, but on 28th June[59] hooters were heard going off all over the place. The war was really over, Germany had now agreed terms and everyone could celebrate. The streets of Stafford were crowded with people including many soldiers who had coloured ribbons in their hats! It was amid these celebrations that the Police decided to ask all drivers to show their licences! There was no such excitement in the Camp but Sir Arthur celebrated at dinner, along with Evie and Captain Thomas of the Royal Irish Regiment, by drinking his last bottle of "Bubbly".

The prisoners still had to be kept occupied as they waited for repatriation so Sir Arthur decided that they

[58] D615/BS/6/10 Staffordshire Record Office.

[59] Treaty of Versailles signed on 28th June, the 5th anniversary of the assassination of Archduke Franz Ferdinand of Austria.

should build a tennis court in front of his quarters. Although he was aware that his days in Staffordshire were soon to come to an end he went ahead with the project saying it would be there for others after he had gone.

By July 1919 it was time for Sir Arthur and his family to leave Brocton and go home to Scotland. In two and a half years they had collected a great deal of "stuff" which required a whole van on the railway, and that did not include the pony trap! Prisoners helped the family pack up as, in the Commandant's opinion, the servants were useless! The cook was caught trying to make off with 2lbs of butter and the orderly had failed to feed, water and groom the ponies as instructed! Evie left for Scotland with the children and their luggage, on the over-night train on 22nd July. Sir Arthur had just a few days left in charge before he handed over the reins and the innumerable lists he had written, to Colonel Bolton, who would be responsible for running the camp until it closed.

Captain & Mrs Levett

Although many prisoners had been repatriated, others were still arriving as their camps were closed down. 237 prisoners arrived from Burbage and

Peak Dale on 23rd July. They had been working in the quarries in Derbyshire and all seemed very fit and weather beaten.

Sir Arthur paid a last visit to Brocton Leys which now looked very lonely and empty. He was to see the owner, Mrs Lees, to discuss any damage for which the family may have been responsible. Mrs Lees was distressed, as her son Charles had inherited over £100,000 on the occasion of his 21st birthday in October 1916, but somehow he had got into the hands of the "Skiver Gang", the worst crooks in London, and they were rapidly removing his fortune.

Sir Arthur's final days were relaxed and spent writing letters, playing tennis, dining with the Levetts at Milford Hall, having a ride in a tank (which nearly made him sick), having his portrait painted in water colours by a prisoner and on 26th July attending a splendid fire-works display in Shug-borough Park. He returned to camp at midnight bringing with him a very drunk soldier!

On 30th July he said goodbye to his staff who, he said, had done him very well. Birley, his faithful adjutant, who had been at his side for the past two and a half years, was given a staff post and there was a letter of appreciation from Colonel Lawrence in York. It was now time to go, driving through Lichfield and on to Coventry for lunch. His time as Commandant of Brocton Prisoner of War Camp was over.

Slowly the Prisoners were repatriated, but in July 1919 the Dundee Courier reported that there were still 91,818 German prisoners of War in Britain. About the same time 1,000 prisoners left Buxton, a satellite camp of Brocton, for

Germany. They had been employed in the limestone industry, and Sir Arthur had made regular visits to their Camp during his time in Brocton. By October 1919 the Camp at Buxton was closed and all the huts sold.

On 14th October 1919, five trains left Milford & Brocton Station loaded with three thousand prisoners on route for Hull on the start of their journey back to Germany. A thousand of them would travel home on S.S. Melilla. The steamer was flying a very worn German flag and its officers also looked tired, worn and anaemic. A soldier in the escort party said of the prisoners "they were leaving with a belly full of good English grub." All that was available for them to eat on the journey was dark German bread. An old field cooker was heating up a liquid of some description - it may have been a drink or even a watery soup!

The German Officers told of strikes all over Germany, and a general disinclination to work. A new suit would cost the equivalent of £50 and butter was thirty shillings a pound. No wonder the prisoners were quiet as they embarked. The Germans stood silent and motionless as the ship floated into the middle of the Humber. They were on their way home at last. Despite all their complaints, would life be any better at home than at Brocton?

Many of the Prisoners sported moustaches in the manner of the Kaiser. They carried with them small mirrors and brushes to keep them in trim. The Hull Daily Mail records how, when on arrival at the Riverside Quay[60] a

[60] The Riverside Quay was completed in 1911 and contained a Passenger Station. Prisoners were transferred straight from the train to their ship.

carriage door was opened to reveal a Hun who was very busy brushing up his moustache with the aid of a little glass.

"Come on out of it you blighter, this is not a barber's shop" a jolly Tommy exclaimed.

Kaiser Wilhelm

Just a week later another 1200 prisoners from Brocton arrived in two trains at the Riverside Docks. They were to sail on the steamship "Bagdad" for Emdon. The trains were more than four hours late arriving, but the Captain was sure that they would be back in Germany by the following evening. Every German, many of whom looked little more than boys, was carefully marked off the list as they boarded the ship. One youth carried a guitar on his back, but most of the others just had a small bag or box containing their personal belongings. The armed guards appeared quite jovial and on friendly terms with the prisoners, but a group of dockers made it quite clear what they thought of the departing prisoners. Their language was ripe, and they viewed the Germans with complete and utter disgust.

On 24th October, 1919, prisoners from Bolsover Castle arrived at Brocton Camp. The Camp at the Castle had been closed Brocton was to be a temporary staging post on their journey home.[61]

As the number of prisoners at Brocton dwindled, the Staffordshire Advertiser on the 29th November, 1919, commented on the valuable work done by the Germans during the previous two years. "Now that the majority of German Prisoners of War have gone home and most of the agricultural camps closed, it is not without interest to consider the work the PoWs did on English Farms. They were first employed in agricultural work in early 1917, and the total number allotted to the Food Production Department varied from time to time. In January 1919 there were 30,679 prisoners so employed throughout the country. They were divided into four classes:-

1) Prisoners working from depots, sent out to the same farm daily and returning to camp to sleep.

2) Prisoners boarded out with farmers. A limited number (1,735) known as Scheme B.

3) 1,008 Prisoners of War sent out daily from Parent Camps.

4) 3,041 working in migratory gangs going where they were needed at a specific time.

15,000 men have been repatriated to date while the remainder are leaving day by day as circumstances permit.

[61] Derbyshire Courier 25.10.1919

At first there was much prejudice amongst farmers, but they were generally regarded as a valuable addition to the local labour in agricultural and drainage operations. It has been good to have them around to help with the 1919 harvest"

Although none of the Germans had wanted to spend time as Prisoners of War, many kept in touch with the farmers they had worked for and were grateful for the treatment they had received whilst in England.

January 1919 had seen the sale of 100 heavy and light draught horses from Brocton and Rugeley Camps. They were sold as soon as they were no longer needed. It required manpower to look after them and valuable pasture land to keep them fed!

In July 1920 the Ministry of Munitions, by direction of the Disposal Board (Furniture Section), were auctioning off at Brocton Camp much of the fixtures and fittings from the Camps.[62] At the same time there was a great sale of Army Huts taking place at Rugeley Camp.

But before all the huts were dismantled a number of boys arrived to spend a holiday on Cannock Chase.[63] Sent by the West Bethnal Green Country Holiday Fund Committee it was the only chance these London children would have of seeing the countryside in its summer splendour. Residents in the area were invited to assist by donating suitable gifts for the boys and perhaps giving up a little time to help entertain them.

[62] A list of some of the items for sale can be found in the appendix.

[63] Lichfield Mercury July 1920.

A Hut at Walton on the Hill,

By the middle of October further huts at Brocton were for sale by private treaty. The disposal of huts continued right up until 1922, and in July of that year the double ovens, cooking ranges and boilers were all available for purchase. Messrs. Winterton and Sons continued to advertise in the Lichfield Mercury. By March 1923 their advertisement included the sale of the following:- steam pumps, pulley and fly wheels, Windsor and arm chairs, 2,000 flag poles, a timber constructed footbridge 52 feet by 4 feet, 500lbs of nails, 70 spanners, 50 picks and a large quantity of tools and other equipment. Their adverts reminded people "that facilities for removing materials purchased are afforded by the military railway which runs nearby." The huts would eventually become homes, shops and village halls throughout the county. When everything had been sold, the land was finally returned to the Earl of Lichfield.

Camp Newspaper Easter 1919.

The war is over and a prisoner looks out towards Milford and the Trent Valley, waiting for the day he will return home.

The route of the Military Railway is still clearly visible and a walk along it is a gentle stroll from Milford to Brocton and then on to the top of the Chase. The lines of the Prisoner of War Camp were situated on either side of the railway but if you walk along the track today there is no obvious trace of the camp which held so many German nationals between 1917 and 1919.

Brocton Coppice 2015

A final footnote & link with the Parish of Berkswich

1921 Leipzig

The Leipzig War Crimes Trials were a series of trials held in 1921 to try alleged German war criminals of the First World War before the German Supreme Court in Leipzig, as part of the penalties imposed on the German government under the Treaty of Versailles.

The following Germans were found guilty of mistreating Prisoners of War.

Sergeant Karl Heynen, charged with mistreating British prisoners of war. He was sentenced to a brief prison term of ten months.

Captain Emil Müller, charged with mistreating prisoners of war. He was sentenced to six months in prison.

Private Robert Neumann, charged with mistreating prisoners of war. He was sentenced to six months in prison.

The trials took place before seven judges but the British Government took no direct part in the proceedings. However, a British mission led by the Solicitor General, Sir Ernest Pollock attended on behalf of the Government. Sir Ernest was a regular visitor to Walton on the Hill and at the Parish Social in December 1915 he had given a talk on "The Great War". He was also often seen performing monologues at concerts held in the village school.

Sir Ernest Pollock, 1st Lord Hanworth

Sir Ernest was son-in-law to Lady Salt who had lived at Weeping Cross with her husband, Sir Thomas Salt, until his death in 1904. Lady Salt then moved to Walton on the Hill where she lived until 1920. Charles Pollock, her grandson, and son of Sir Ernest, had been killed in France on 31st March, 1918.

Appendix 1

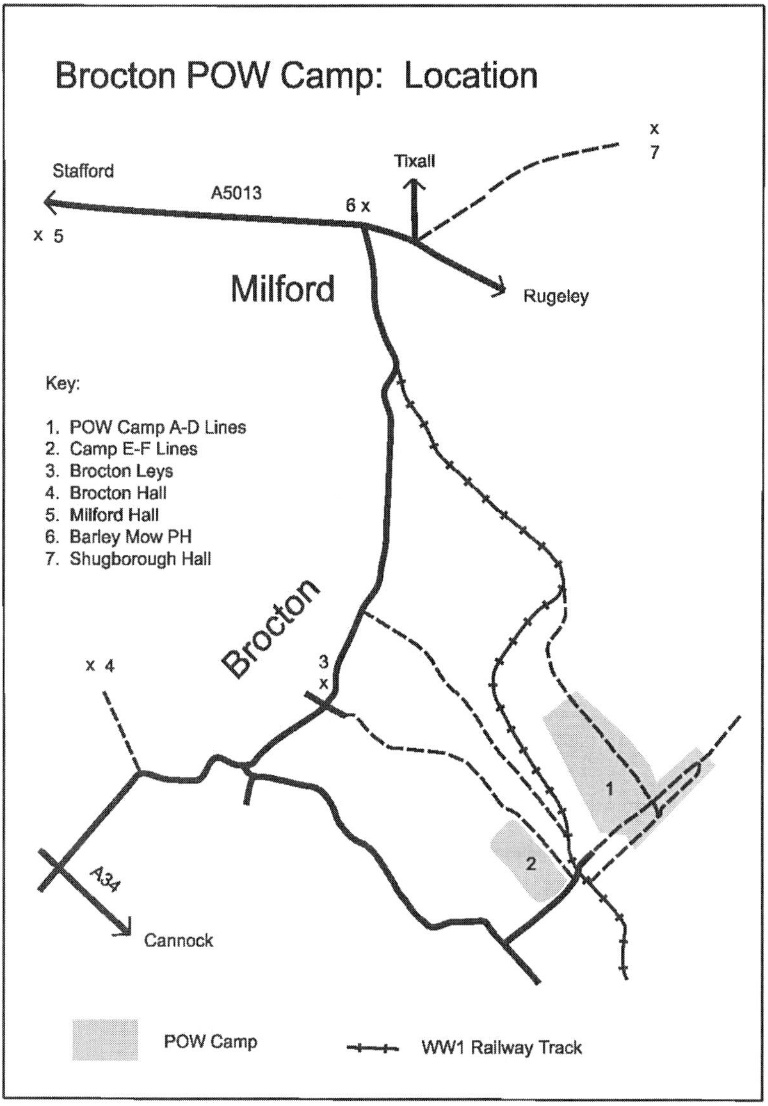

For a more detailed map of the area see the OS Explorer 244 Map of Cannock Chase, including Stafford, Rugeley & Cannock.

Appendix 2

PoW Camps under Brocton's Control in 1917-

Healeyfield, Co. Durham
Stanhope, Co. Durham
Eastgate, Co Durham,
Harperley, Co Durham
Port Clarence, Middlesborough
Sproxton Moor, Nr Malton, Yorks.
Coal Aston, Sheffield
Catterick, Yorks.
Slaley, Northumberland
Uppingham, Rutlandshire,
Peak Dale, Derbyshire opened on 3.4.17
Burbage Buxton opened on 28.5.17
Bilston opened on 23.5.17
Grantham, Lincs.
Sutton Bridge
South Carlton

On January 1st 1918, Catterick was made a Parent Camp and the following Camps were transferred to its care :- Healeyfield, Stanhope, Eastgate, Harperley, Port Clarence, Sproxton Moor, Coal Aston and Slaley.

The following Camps were opened after Brocton was established-
Denby, Derby opened on 15.9.17
Boston Dock (Aliens) opened on 30.10.17
Stainby (Aliens) opened on 19.1.18
Burton on Trent opened on 20.1.18
Bracebridge opened on 25.3.18
Ashbourne opened on 25.3.18
Crich, Matlock opened on 22.7.18

In 1918 Agricultural Depots were set up to meet the demand for Prisoner of War labour. Nine were opened under the control of Brocton –

Loughborough
Market Harborough
Kelham
Croxton Park
Wainfleet
Sleaford
Plumtree
Retford
Grantham

The following are smaller Agricultural Camps under Brocton's control:-

Ashby-de-la Zouche, Leics; Bretby, Derbs; Bucknall, Lincs; Burton Hall, Lincs; Caythorpe, Lincs: Chapel-en-le-Frith, Derbys; Coningsby, Lincs; Digby, Lincs; East Leake, Lincs; Etwall, Derbys; Grindley on the Hill, Lincs; Houghton on the Hill, Leics: Ilkeston, Derbys;Illstone, Leics: Folkingham, Lincs; Glentham, Lincs; Great Hale, Lincs; Hogsthorpe, Lincs: Holbeach, Lincs: Laneham, Notts: Long Clawson, Leics; Morton, Lincs: Narborugh, Leics; Normanton, Lincs: North Kilworth, Warks; Norton Cuckney, Notts; Osbournby, Lincs: Papplewick, Notts; Partney, Lincs; Ragdale Hall, Leics; Ranskill, Yorks; Rippingale, Lincs; Somerby Hall, Lincs; Stone, Staffs; Stow Park, Lincs; Sudbury, Derbys; Temple Bruer, Lincs; Thorpe Satchville, Leics; Timberland, Lincs; Tuxford, Notts; Uttoxeter, Staffs; Willington, Derby; Woodborough, Notts: Wrottesley, Staffs; Wymondham, Leics.

Appendix 3

How the Spanish Influenza Epidemic Affected the Brocton Prisoner of War Camp.

Year	1917	1918	1919
January	Camp did not Open until April	1	13
February		0	4
March		0	7
April	0	0	0
May	2	5	4
June	3	3	5
July	1	2	1
August	1	8	0
September	3	11	1
October	2	28	1
November	1	65	2
December	2	24	0
Total Deaths in the Year	15	148	39

All deaths did not occur because of the influenza epidemic but it had a serious impact on prisoners, especially those already suffering from other complaints & injuries

Appendix 4
Prisoner Deaths at Brocton 1917 – 1919

This list was compiled by visiting the Cannock Chase War Cemetery and comparing the names of those buried there with deaths registered in Stafford during 1917 – 1919.

The 58 German burials in Plot 4 were all brought into the cemetery in 1963, as part of the German Government's policy to remove all graves situated in cemeteries or war graves plots not maintained by the Commonwealth War Graves Commission. These deaths are not registered in Stafford but in many different part of the country as far afield as Newcastle upon Tyne in the north and Chichester in the south. We can therefore assume that the following Germans, buried in Plot 3, whose deaths were registered in Stafford, were Prisoners of War on the Chase.

Surname	**First name**	**Age**	**Date of Death**
ABRAHAM	Martin	23	27.6.19
AKKERMANN	Theodor	37	14.8.18
ALBERT	Alfons	29	29.4.18
ALBRECHT	Wilhelm	23	21.1.19
ALBRECHT	Hermann	31	25.10.18
BACHERT	Jakob	31	24.11.18
BALZER	Franz	37	16.3.19
BARTELS	Wilhelm	19	14.1.19
BAUER	Rudolf	26	5.11.18
BEBBER	Wilhelm Van	20	6.12.18
BECKER	Fritz	28	22.11.18

BECKER	Friedrich	37	17.11.18
BECKER	Jacob	29	28.5.19
BERGMANN	Josef	21	4.12.18
BIRCK	Arnold	34	21.5.19
BISCHOFF	Albert	25	23.1.19
BODDIKER	Heinrich	24	17.7.18
BODNER	August	33	5.11.19
BOHME	Rudolf	24	11.11.18
BOLEK	Gustav	20	5.3.19
BORG	Julius	20	14.11.18
BRIESKE	Ernst	38	17.11.18
BRUDLO	Adolph	21	18.5.18
BRUGGERMAN	Max	22	10.6.18
BUCHBERGER	Johann	34	16.2.19
BUCKECKER	Karl	32	6.2.19
BUHR	Heinrich	19	27.12.18
BUNGE	Johannes	22	19.8.18
BUNGER	August	29	4.12.18
CARLE	Heinrich	23	31.12.18
CARSTENS	Claus	28	23.7.17
DEHMELT	Wilhelm	19	24.11.19
DICKMANN	Heinrich	27	10.8.18
DIETL	Josef	34	9.6.19
DIETRICH	Karl	24	18.12.18
DOMBROWSKI	Felix	23	16.11.18
DUMONT	Baptiste	28	11.9.18
DWENGER	Wilheln	19	17.10.18
DYBALLA	Theodor	36	19.11.18
DZIADZKA	Edward	29	13.5.18
EICHMANN	Otto	22	7.5.19
ERNST	Wilhelm	27	1.12.17

FINKE	Bernhard	22	6.11.18
FRUBRICK	Walter	19	29.6.19
FUCHS	Oskar	27	1.11.18
FULLE	Johann	33	21.9.18
GALINSKI	Karl	34	14.11.18
GALLAR	Emil	22	23.12.18
GEIZZLER	Artur (Max)	44	11.9.18
GIERTZ	Ernst	21	4.5.18
GLAUBERT	Boleslaw	24	30.10.18
GOEBEL	William	20	8.6.17
GRASSLIN	Friedrich	29	23.11.18
GRIEBEL	Paul	21	25.10.18
GRIMM	Frederich	34	11.10.18
GROSSE	Johannes	21	28.10.18
GROSSLAUB	Theodor	38	2.9.18
GUNSKE	Adolf	23	7.1.19
GUST	Erich	19	26.12.18
HAASE	Theodor Max	31	22.11.18
HADRICH	Paul	20	5.1.19
HAGL	Anton	28	30.10.18
HANNIG	Herbert (Karl)	20	13.10.18
HANSEN	Fogt Peter	24	18.10.18
HANSEN	Peter	26	22.5.17
HANSEN	Carston	33	14.11.18
HASSE	Theodor	31	22.11.18
HEGER	Alfred	25	30.9.18
HEINEMANN	Wilhelm	24	28.10.17
HILLER	Johannes	21	3.5.19
HINRICHE	Hermann	23	14.9.18
HOLTFRETER	Paul	23	27.10.18
HORNER	Jakob	34	1.1.19

HUNERSDORFF	Hermann von	42	8.11.18
IKENMAYER	Conra	20	15.11.17
JACOB	Andreis	26	15.11.18
JAGER	Willy	21	3.7.19
JAGER	Vinzenz	25	3.11.18
JANOTTA	Franz	20	15.8.17
JERZEWSKI	Bruno	25	26.11.18
JUST	Otto	19	18.11.18
KABOLLECK	Karl	20`	27.2.19
KAMPMEYER	Wilhelm	25	30.11.18
KESSEN	Heinrich	31	12.6.19
KIRCHENSTEINER	Josef	37	30.9.18
KIRCHNER	George	35	12.11.18
KLAMM	Fritz	30	11.3.19
KLEIBUSCH	Willy	21	22.10.18
KLEMM	Ernst	47	9.9.19
KLINGENBERG	Herman	19	28.8.18
KLOTZSCH	Paul	25	31.3.19
KNIPPER	Heinrich	29	3.12.18
KOHLER	Otto	33	8.12.18
KOPF	Rudolf	23	1.11.18
KORLIN	Wilhelm	22	7.11.18
KOSTER	Johann	22	23.10.18
KRAFT	Georg	26	26.10.19
KRAMER	Wilhelm	28	15.6.17
KRATTE	Johannes	38	28.10.18
KRAUS	Johann	26	28.11.18
KRIENKE	Paul	19	22.11.18
KUHN	Freidrich	21	9.1.19
KUNT	Franz	20	14.6.19
LANG	Georg Emil	21	29.1.19

LANGER	Carl	28	22.5.18
LETZ	Hermann	33	9.12.18
LICH	Wilhelm	21	8.1.19
LIND	Karl	27	22.8.18
LIPPOLD	Jacob	25	12.6.18
LOCHER	Hermann	22	7.12.18
LORENZ	Alfred	21	2.12.18
LUCAS	Karl	20	27.10.18
MALEK	Wladistaua	19	7.10.18
METZGER	Josef	29	4.11.18
MEYER	Dietrich	39	6.3.19
MEYER	Josef	38	24.11.18
MICHEL	Georg	18	29.10.18
MISCH	Josef	20	26.11.18
MITTENZWEI	Kurt	21	21.1.19
MOES	Friedrich	21	3.12.18
MOLLER	Bruno	19	22.8.18
MROWEZYNSKI	Johann	32	26.9.17
MULLER	Alois	22	30.1.19
NAGEL	Fritz	20	7.11.18
NAGELE	Hermann	20	31.10.18
NEUTE	Ernst	20	25.10.18
NICKEL	Peter	30	31.10.18
NIKLAUS	Hermann	19	12.12.18
NIXDORF	Franz	27	6.12.18
PATHKE	Theodor	23	22.11.18
PAUL	Karl	39	26.11.18
PETZET	Georg	28	29.6.18
PFAU	Johannes	19	26.10.18
PIEPER	Richard	40	27.11.18
PIPER	Richard F.W.	21	18.12.18

POCHERER	Paul	25	9.11.18
POVALLA	Emil	19	19.10.18
PRESCHER	Max	24	20.10.18
PUSCH	Paul	32	11.1.19
RAPPE	Georg	26	3.11.18
RAUCH	Christian	28	9.11.18
REICH	Vinzent	28	20.10.18
REIGRUBER	Leonhardt	29	12.11.18
RENTMEISTER	Heinrich	21	5.1.18
RICHTER	Gustav	25	1.2.19
RODEL	Oskar	31	26.11.18
ROGGENBUCK	Ernst	22	30.11.18
ROMAINSKI	Franz	31	27.9.18
ROSENBAUM	Peter	31	18.8.18
ROSLER	Robert	26	28.11.18
ROSSBERG	Otto	33	12.12.18
ROTHE	Karl	22	26.11.18
RUDEL	Ernst	42	25.11.18
RZESWITZEK	Emil	25	4.11.18
SANDKANS	Peter	21	2.5.18
SATORIUS	Josef	23	8.11.18
SAUERBORN	Peter	27	17.11.18
SCHATLEIN	Andreas	40	11.1.19
SCHILLER	Arno	19	16.10.18
SCHLEICHER	Hugo	22	11.12.17
SCHMALIX	Ernst	21	1.11.18
SCHMIDT	Franz	21	21.5.17
SCHMUDDE	Wilhelm	21	18.11.18
SCHOBER	Johann	28	12.12.18
SCHULZE	Otto	19	3.1.19
SCHULZE	Otto	19	23.12.18

SECHSER	Simon	23	31.10.18
SEIDEL	Albert	23	27.11.18
SIEBEN	Johann	22	10.6.17
SKLAREK	Albert	22	12.11.18
SKUBSCH	August	30	20.11.18
SLADEK	Johann	24	6.12.18
SOMMER	Paul	19	16.11.18
SOPORA	Anton	31	2.12.18
SPINDLER	August	19	7.11.18
STANKE	Herman	21	22.11.18
STEIB	Adam	35	2.8.18
STEINECKE	Phillipp	20	11.9.18
STRAUSS	Siegfried	22	23.12.18
TEGEN	Willy	20	21.10.17
THIEL	Edwald	23	22.10.18
THIEL	Gregor	25	16.11.18
TINGS	August	24	3.3.19
TRENKEL	Max	19	26.3.19
TSCHECH	Fritz	22	23.10.18
VECKER	Wilhelm	27	11.11.18
VOGEL	Alfred	26	17.10.18
VOLKNER	Karl	33	20.11.18
VOSSKUHLER	Fritz	26	25.11.18
WALDECK	Ernest	28	26.11.18
WEBER	Ferdinand	37	29.9.18
WEIDENBRUCH	Hermann	26	2.11.18
WEINGARTNER	Joseph	39	1.11.18
WEISSHAUPT	Adolf	23	2.12.18
WELSCH	Richard	20	19.9.18
WESTPHAL	Friedrich	33	19.10.18
WERNER	August	21	17.9.17

WIMMELMEIR	Adam	22	24.9.17
WINKLER	Edmand	22	3.7.18
WOLKE	Karl	18	25.10.18
WOROCK	Franz	27	11.11.18
WROBEL	Franz	29	25.11.18
WYSOTZKI	Leo von	29	7.5.19
ZANDER	Ferdinand	34	9.11.18

Appendix 5

Sale of Fittings from Brocton Camp

Ministry of Munitions

By Direction of the Disposal Board (Furniture Section)

Sale by Auction

At the Ordnance Depot, Brocton Camp,

Monday & Tuesday 26 & 27 July, 1920

355 Iron bedsteads	838 Bedside Tables
245 Chests of Drawers	238 Painted washstands
74 Wardrobes	109 Hair stuffed Lounge Chairs
1684 Windsor & other chairs	214 Upholstered Chairs
51 Deal & other tables	548 Deal Forms
333 Trestle Table Tops	840 Iron Trestles
900 Bill Hooks	32 Invalid's wheeling chairs

84 Costly ward tables with tile and enamelled tops
Earthenware, glass, baskets, brushes, mirrors,
straw & mill boards
Catalogues available from Evans & Evans,
Greengate Street, Stafford.

Whether these items came from the Prisoner of War Camp or from other parts of Brocton & Rugeley Camps we cannot tell. The sales continued until 1923 when eventually all the equipment required to house and feed thousands of soldiers during 1915 – 1920 had been disposed of.

Appendix 6

Currency in 1917

Farthing		one quarter of a penny
Halfpenny		half of a penny, 480 in a pound
Penny	1d	twelve to a shilling
Florin	2/-	two shilling piece, now 10p
Halfcrown	2/6	Two shillings and six pence
One Pound	£1	A bank note equalling 240 pence or 20 shillings.

Appendix 7

Bibliography

Down Memory Lane	Complied by Jim Foley
Stands the Church Clock	Dyonese Haszard
Memories – Berkswich in the Great War	Berkswich History Society
Down by Jacob's Ladder	Laura Husslbee
Prisoners of War in British Hands during WW1	Graham Mark
Prisoners of Britain	Panikos Panayi
Barbed wire disease. British & German Prisoners of War 1914-19	John Yarnall
100 Years of Golf	K. Davey/N. Griffiths
A Childhood in Scotland	Christian Miller
The Diaries of Sir Arthur Grant	Unpublished
Hansard	
Various newspapers including -	

- Aberdeen Journal
- Birmingham Post
- Hull Daily Mail
- Lichfield Mercury
- London Gazette
- Staffordshire Advertiser
- Stafford Newsletter

Appendix 8

Acknowledgements

I must extend my grateful thanks to the following people who have all helped to make this book possible.

Sir Archibald & Lady Fiona Grant of Monymusk
Mrs Virginia Grant of Kingstone Bagpuzie
Anne Andrews of Ingestre & Tixall History Society
Dr M. Cox for several photographs of Brocton Prisoners
John Haddon for help with German translation.
Marion Kettle of the Landor Society
Graham Mark for photograph of the Football team
Bob Morton for help with preparing the book for printing
Peter Mynors for permission to quote Wm Mynors diary
Doug Peel for interpretation & drawing of Maps.
Christopher Phillips for photo of Brocton Leys
Richard Purshouse of "The Chase Project "
Tom Wyre for permission to reproduce his poem "POW"

Staff of the following organisations:-
William Salt Library, Stafford;
Staffordshire Record Office;
Imperial War Museum, London;
National Archives, Kew;
National Records of Scotland, Edinburgh.
British Museum

All friends too numerous to name individually, who have helped with ideas and proof reading.

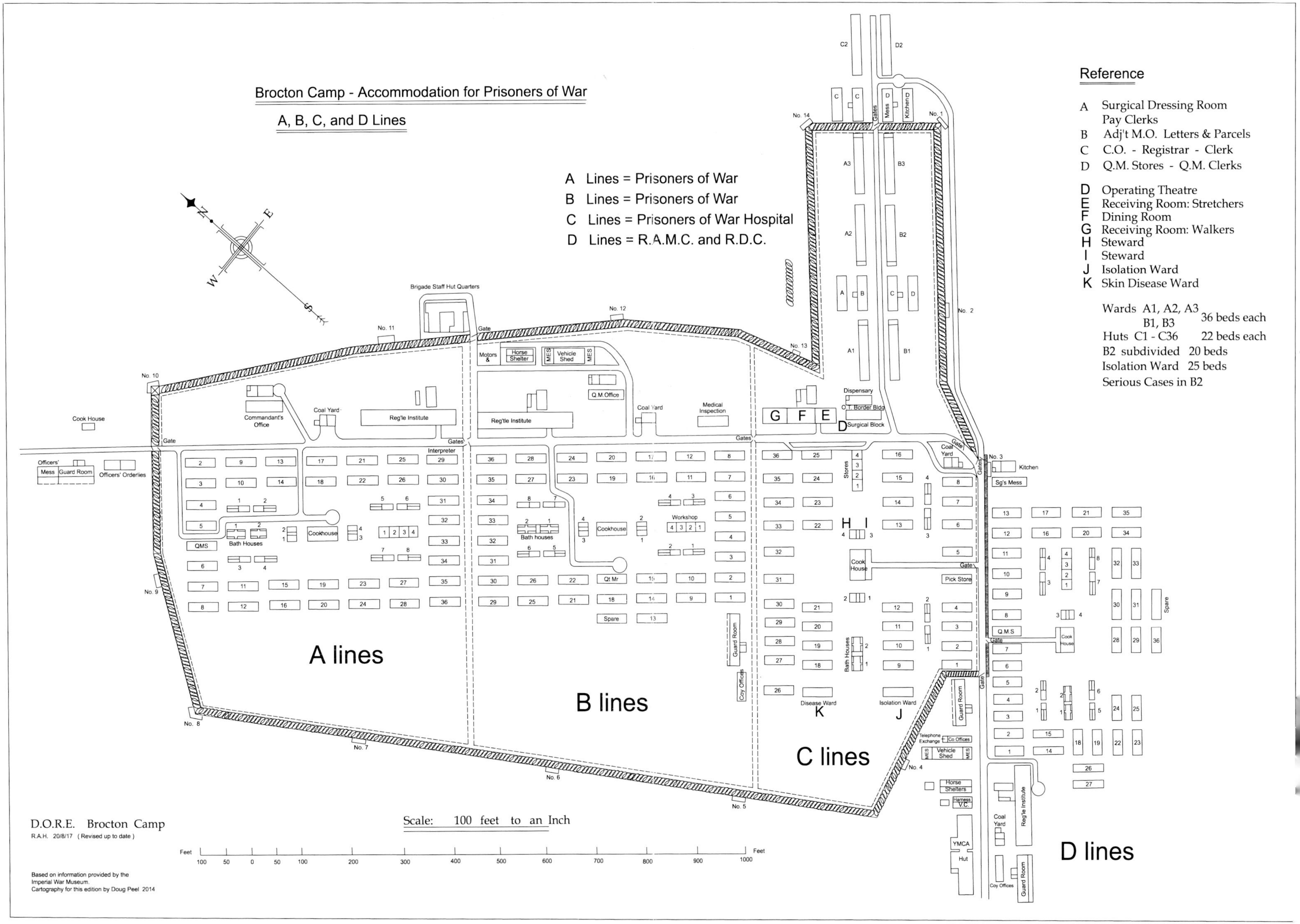
Brocton Camp - Accommodation for Prisoners of War
A, B, C, and D Lines
A Lines = Prisoners of War
B Lines = Prisoners of War
C Lines = Prisoners of War Hospital
D Lines = R.A.M.C. and R.D.C.
Reference
A Surgical Dressing Room
Pay Clerks
B Adj't M.O. Letters & Parcels
C C.O. - Registrar - Clerk
D Q.M. Stores - Q.M. Clerks
D Operating Theatre
E Receiving Room: Stretchers
F Dining Room
G Receiving Room: Walkers
H Steward
I Steward
J Isolation Ward
K Skin Disease Ward
Wards A1, A2, A3 B1, B3 36 beds each
Huts C1 - C36 22 beds each
B2 subdivided 20 beds
Isolation Ward 25 beds
Serious Cases in B2
A lines
B lines
C lines
D lines
Brigade Staff Hut Quarters
Commandant's Office
Coal Yard
Reg'tle Institute
Cook House
Officers' Mess
Guard Room
Officers' Orderlies
Bath Houses
Cookhouse
QMS
Interpreter
Motors &
Horse Shelter
Vehicle Shed
Q.M.Office
Medical Inspection
Dispensary
O.T. Border Bldg
Surgical Block
Workshop
Qt Mr
Spare
Coy Offices
Stores
Disease Ward
Isolation Ward
Pick Store
Kitchen
Sg's Mess
Q.M.S
Telephone Exchange
Co Offices
Horse Shelters
Harness
V.C.
YMCA
Hut
Scale: 100 feet to an Inch
Feet 100 50 0 50 100 200 300 400 500 600 700 800 900 1000 Feet
D.O.R.E. Brocton Camp
R.A.H. 20/8/17 (Revised up to date)
Based on information provided by the
Imperial War Museum.
Cartography for this edition by Doug Peel 2014